# HISTOIRE

## NATURELLE

## *DES INDES*

*W · W · NORTON & COMPANY*

*New York · London*

# HISTOIRE
## NATURELLE
# *DES INDES*

---

The
*Drake Manuscript*
*in The*
*Pierpont Morgan Library*

*Preface by Charles E. Pierce, Jr.*
*Foreword by Patrick O'Brian*
*Introduction by Verlyn Klinkenborg*
*Translations by Ruth S. Kraemer*

Copyright © 1996 by The Pierpont Morgan Library
Foreword copyright © 1996 by Patrick O'Brian
Introduction copyright © 1996 by Verlyn Klinkenborg

Photography by David A. Loggie,
The Pierpont Morgan Library

The text of this book is composed in Poliphilus
with the display set in Blado
Book design and composition by Antonina Krass
Manufacturing by Balding + Mansell, Peterborough, England

ISBN 0-393-03994-3

W. W. Norton & Company, Inc., 500 Fifth Avenue, New York, N.Y. 10110
http://www.wwnorton.com
W. W. Norton & Company Ltd., 10 Coptic Street, London WC1A 1PU

1 2 3 4 5 6 7 8 9 0

# CONTENTS

# PREFACE

When the Drake Manuscript, as it has often been called, or *Histoire Naturelle des Indes,* as it was entitled when it was bound, came to The Pierpont Morgan Library in 1983, it provoked considerable excitement. As a bequest of Miss Clara S. Peck, it was a splendid addition to the Library's collection of literature related to the European discovery of the Americas. Its two specific references to Sir Francis Drake and its references to many of his known ports of call, its 400-year absence from public view, the range of its portraiture and the charm of its drawings—all contributed to the strong interest we felt and continue to feel.

Until now, the manuscript has been accessible to a very few. It has been studied by researchers who visited the Library and, from time to time, shown to the public in exhibitions. Single leaves have been reproduced in a variety of publications. Here, though, for the first time, all the drawings and their captions are available in a facsimile edition. General readers, as well as specialists, can enjoy and study a manuscript, exceptional in beauty and rich in history.

Charles E. Pierce, Jr.
Director, The Pierpont Morgan Library

# FOREWORD
## by Patrick O' Brian

Francis Drake began life with a fine resounding name, but nothing more; for although he was related to the ship-owning Hawkins family of Plymouth, and although his father, a man of obscure origins, took care to beg a great noble, Francis Russell, to stand sponsor for him when he was baptized, nobody seems to have done anything for him when he was a child: even his best biographers have no information about his schooling.

The earliest account I have of him is that of his contemporary, William Camden, the historian and antiquary, who says:

> This Drake (to relate no more than what I have heard from himself) was born of mean parentage in Devonshire, and had Francis Russel (afterwards Earl of Bedford) for his Godfather, who, according to Custome, gave him his christian name. Whilest he was yet a Child, his Father imbracing the Protestant Doctrine, was called in question by the Law of the Six articles, made by King Henry the Eighth against the Protestants, fled his Countrey, and withdrew himself into Kent. After the death of King Henry he got a place among the sea-men in the King's Navy, to reade Prayers to them: and soon after he was ordained Deacon, and made Vicar of the Church of Upnore upon the River Medway (the Road where the Fleet usually anchoreth). But by reason of his Poverty, he put his son to the Master of a Bark, his neighbour, who held him hard to his business in the Bark, with which he used to coast along the

Shoar, and sometimes to carry Marchandize into Zeland and France. The Youth being painful and diligent, so pleased the Old Man by his industry, that being a bachelour, at his death he bequeathed the Bark unto him by Will and Testament.

Here, then, was Francis Drake set up, and for some time he carried on with his calling; but in the early 1560's he joined one or two of the Hawkins slaving voyages, which brought him acquainted with the Guinea Coast and the Spanish West Indies. In 1567 he sailed with the formidable John Hawkins himself in a fleet of six vessels, the flagship being the aged *Jesus of Lubeck*, 700 tons, lent by Queen Elizabeth, who also provided the *Minion* (this was a mercantile venture in which she took part as a private person). The idea was to fill up with blacks, bought or captured, and to sell them in the West Indies or on the Spanish Main—an illegal trade by Spanish law but one that with proper bribery and a show of force could be carried on very profitably. By February 1568 they had about 400 slaves, and with them they crossed the Atlantic to Dominica: at this time Drake was in command of the *Judith*, about fifty tons. They traded along the coast with moderate success until they reached Rio de la Hacha. Drake had been sent ahead to open negotiations. He was answered with gunfire: this he returned, and stood off to wait for Hawkins, who dealt with the Spaniards' reluctance by storming the town and burning most of it. They moved on, with some success at Santa Marta but none at all at the well-fortified Cartagena, and then shaped their course for home before the hurricane season.

But in August, when they were off Cuba, heading for Florida and the Atlantic westerlies, they met with an appalling four-day blow which so shattered the *Jesus* that they had to cut down her upper works: her rudder was much shaken and she had a very dangerous leak. They found no shelter on the coast of Florida, and another storm blew them right across the Gulf of Mexico and down that of Campeche, where, after a month of incessant pumping, they took refuge in San Juan de Ulloa.

The local officials made no objection to Hawkins's entry with his ships: indeed, the harbour guns even fired a salute, it being thought that the vessels were an advance party from the expected Spanish fleet, bringing the new viceroy. When the officials came aboard Hawkins pacified them with promises: all he wanted to do was to repair his ships—he had no other aims at all. The Spanish fleet appeared next morning. Hawkins sent civil messages (England and Spain were at peace), proposing an exchange of hostages. He also set up a battery on the island of San Juan. The viceroy sent an amiable reply, and a trumpet-blast signified his agreement. Two days after the Spanish fleet had worked into the harbour they began their carefully-prepared attack. A very furious action followed, in which one Spanish ship was blown up, another burnt, and another sunk. The *Jesus* was disabled: other English ships were fired or sent to the bottom. Hawkins moved into the *Minion* with most of his treasure, and both he and Drake in the *Judith* moved out of range and anchored, knotting and splicing. In the night the *Judith* disappeared, but the two ships reached home within a few days of one another; and although Drake's enemies sometimes held this disappearance against him, Hawkins bore no lasting grudge. They sailed together in the fleet that conquered the Armada, and again in yet another expedition against the Spaniards in the West Indies.

Yet although Hawkins may not have blamed him, it has been suggested that Drake blamed himself, converting much of this powerful emotion into a still more bitter hatred for the Spaniards which was probably his most important spring of action and which legitimized all his subsequent enterprises; though a love for gold and a loathing for Catholics had a not inconsiderable influence—he was after all brought up in a strongly Protestant atosphere: he nearly always sailed with a chaplain and there were frequent prayers and psalm-singing in his ships. Harassing the Spaniards became his way of life; and if any justification were needed, the viceroy's treachery at San Juan de Ulloa provided it in abundance.

Other voyages followed, sometimes with French allies, and Drake came to know the West Indies and the shores of the Spanish Main quite intimately; yet it was not until he made friends with the cimarrons, the black slaves who had run away from their owners and who lived wild, that he beheld the New World in all its true novelty and splendour—the New World with which this glorious manuscript is concerned. For in one particular raid a cimarron chief named Pedro led him far inland through the hot steamy jungle and forest until they came to that famous tall tree at a point so high on the isthmus of Panama that from the platform near its top he could see the Pacific before him, and if he turned, the Atlantic behind; and not only the Pacific but Panama itself, where the treasure-ships brought the wealth of Chile and Peru to be loaded on to mule-trains for the journey across the mountains to Nombre de Dios. Indeed, it was one of these mule-trains that Drake, his men and his French companions hoped to ambush. The ambush failed because a drunken sailor made a noise some moments too soon; but it was clear to Drake that his fortune, and his revenge, lay westward, on those vast waters of the Great South Sea, the Pacific Ocean.

Yet perhaps, before leaving this hot, generally very humid country (80°F the average temperature, with 125 inches of rain a year), a stronghold of malaria, dysentery and yellow fever, I may be allowed a few words on its delights: for delights there were in plenty, outweighing the disadvantage of mosquitoes and other insects (sometimes indescribably troublesome), and they included not only the quetzal bird with its splendid tail but thousands of others, ranging from the gigantic stork *Mycteria americana* to the minute *Steganura underwoodi*, tiny even for a humming-bird (Costa Rica alone has more than twice as many species as the whole of Europe); both the three-toed and the two-toed sloths, jaguars, pumas, the ocelot (often kept as a pet), very large migratory vampires, the manatee in many of the rivers, skunks, and countless orchids—cattleyas, ondontoglossum, miltonia, oncidium . . .

But the illustrators of this manuscript were neither botanists nor biologists: they drew and painted almost entirely from hearsay, and although the animal section has the charm of the later unmoralizing bestiaries and books of wonders, it adds little to the sum of knowledge. On the other hand, the proper study of mankind is man, and here the artists come into their own. They had quite certainly seen Indians in great number, fine upstanding brown Indians: it is the pictures of them fishing, gardening, paddling their canoes, making fire, washing their children, courting their sweethearts and in general living a reasonable, colourful life that gives this book a great deal of its value.

These were the Indians with whom Drake was so familiar, and this the country: but it was the Pacific that was to be his fortune, and returning to England much richer than he left it in spite of missing the mule-train, he assembled a little fleet for the South Sea voyage: the *Pelican* of 150 tons, built to his order, and four others, all smaller. The crews amounted to 164 seamen and boys; but Drake also took several young men of good family, including the brothers Thomas and John Doughty. Why he did this is very far from clear, for he never seems to have been at ease with those of higher rank, and whenever he shared a command with one he was sure to fall out with him.

The voyage was arduous, of course: with the ships, the provisions, the primitive charts and navigational instruments of the time it could not have been otherwise, and it is scarcely worth mentioning the various perils in this place—the routine shortage of water, the uncounted seals eaten off the River Plate, or the three thousand penguins in Magellan's Strait; but Drake's treatment of Thomas Doughty is something else again. There was ill-feeling between them even before the ships left Africa; it increased during the voyage across the ocean, and Drake apparently came to believe that Doughty was plotting against him. When the fleet reached St Julian's, an anchorage on the desolate Patagonian shore, he summoned a court, asserting that the Queen's commission gave him the right to punish sedition with death. Drake was the judge, his subordinates the jury: they decided against Doughty and he was given two days to prepare for execution. On the second day he and Drake took the Eucharist together and dined together. Then after some prayers Doughty knelt to the block, and his head was struck off with an axe.

Samuel Johnson, one of the very few men of his or of later generations to look upon Drake with a cold eye, says of this trial, in which it was alleged that the 'plot' had been concocted in Plymouth, 'How far it is probable . . . that Doughty, who is represented as a man of eminent abilities, should engage in so long and hazardous a voyage with no other view than that of defeating it, is left to the determination of the reader.'

The passage of Magellan's Strait, during which Drake changed his ship's name to the *Golden Hind*, was comparatively easy, but once they were through the weather turned very foul indeed, with furious winds and towering seas that scattered the fleet, driving them far to the south. The *Hind* and the *Elizabeth* reached the western end of the strait again nearly a month later, but the next day the *Elizabeth* was driven back into it. She sailed for home and the *Hind* carried on alone, carrying out an uninterrupted and extraordinarily successful voyage up the coast of Chile and Peru, sacking the towns and pillaging the unprepared Spaniards with such extreme zeal and pertinacity that Drake's name—El Draque or El Draco—became terrible to them.

Right up the coast he went, as far along California as 38°N, where he careened his ship and where, in apparent agreement with an Indian chief of those parts, he annexed the country for his Queen, calling it Nova Albion. After a northward search as far as perhaps 48°N it became clear there was no obvious north-east passage home: nor was it possible to return along the now fully-prepared South American coast. The *Golden Hind* therefore steered for the East Indies, the Cape of Good Hope, and so to Plymouth; and in spite of a brief grounding in the Celebes they accomplished this prodigious voyage, dropping anchor in their home port on 26 September 1580, having first set sail on 15 November 1577.

Their arrival in England caused an immense sensation: the Queen knighted Sir Francis on the deck of the *Golden Hind* and caused her to be laid up in a Deptford creek 'for a monument to all posterity of the famous and worthy exploit.'

This, with another full-hearted raid on the West Indies and the legendary 'singeing of the King of Spain's beard'—the burning of some ten thousand tons of shipping in Cadiz, which delayed the sailing of the Armada—made it obvious that Drake should be given high command when the huge Spanish fleet eventually appeared, in 1588; and Lord High Admiral Howard gave him, Hawkins and Frobisher each a squadron. In the well-named *Revenge* Drake certainly battered the Spaniards most heartily; but in spite of the legend he did not defeat them single-handed, nor anything like it. Indeed, on this occasion too his conduct aroused vehement protest. At one point in the confused battle it was understood that by night, he, with a great stern-lantern, should keep close to the enemy to show the English where they were and to allow the Queen's fleet to keep station. But then the enemy vanished in the darkness; the English fell into disorder; and no light was seen, for the very good reason that *Revenge* had turned back to capture the disabled *Nuestra Señora del Rosario*, remove her heavy pay-chests, and send her in to Torbay. Of course, Drake played his full part in the later action and in pursuing the enemy into the North Sea, and his popular fame mounted highter still. But the *Rosario* stuck in many a naval gullet; and Frobisher, one of the most distinguished sailors of his age, said that Drake 'reporteth that no man hath done so good service as he, but he lyeth in his teeth.'

The end was sad, as most ends are, perhaps: Drake had grown more and more intolerant of differing opinion, and after some unsatisfactory actions on Spanish ports in which he as usual disagreed with the commander of the land forces, he and Hawkins set out on yet another expedition to the West Indies. Here again the two leaders fell out: the long, slow campaign was unsuccessful, for although they took Nombre de Dios the tropical rains made it impossible to cross the isthmus to Panama. They sailed away for Nicaragua, many hands being unwell: off the island of Escudo Drake fell sick with dysentery; and off Porto Bello he died; more, it was thought, of grief than of his disease.

Yet his name lives on; and William Borough's words, written at the end of the six-teenth century, are as valid at the end of the twentieth as they were at that time: 'So now at length our countriman Sir Francis Drake, for valorous prudent proceeding and fortune performing his voyage about the world, is not only become equall to any of them that live, but in fame far surpassing.'

Patrick O'Brian

# INTRODUCTION
## by Verlyn Klinkenborg

In 1983, the Morgan Library received, as the bequest of Clara S. Peck, a manuscript on paper of 134 leaves, bound in eighteenth-century blue morocco. Though this work is often called the Drake Manuscript, it bears on its title page (inserted when it was bound) the name *Histoire Naturelle des Indes*—The Natural History of the Indies. That is an accurate account of its contents, for the volume contains 199 separate images of West Indian plants, animals, and Indian life with accompanying captions written in late sixteenth-century French. *Histoire Naturelle des Indes* did not enter the public record until it was offered for sale in London by Quaritch in 1867. It spent the next eighty years in the libraries of Henry Huth and C. F. G. R. Schwerdt and was acquired by Miss Peck in 1947. It had awaited another thirty-six years before becoming available to scholars at the Morgan Library.

In the mid-1980s, a team of experts scrutinized the Drake Manuscript, hoping to decipher its secrets. They identified most of the locations it mentions, and also identified, in some cases quite precisely, the plants and animals pictured in its drawings. They discovered a possible early owner of the manuscript, l'abbé Jean-Paul Bignon (1662–1743), a French royal librarian whose name may appear in one of the work's margins. And they found, to their surprise, that the Drake Manuscript makes an extraordinary contribution to our knowledge of sixteenth-century French.

To a nautical Protestant like Francis Drake, the Caribbean was irresistible, a natural theater of ambition. Certainly, by 1573 no Englishman knew the region better. There he encountered Indians and "many strange birds, beasts and fishes, besides fruits, trees, plants, and the like," as one of his crew wrote. Drake was alive to the interest of such things, for he was also an artist. Unfortunately, his paintings have been destroyed by the odds that govern the fate of historical artifacts. But sometime probably in the early 1590s, someone thoroughly versed in the Caribbean, created the remarkable gathering of images and text that has come down to us as the Drake Manuscript. Its drawings are often naive but they have a rude vigor, and together with their captions they form the rarest of discoveries: a new window on a new world. And while we can't know exactly the way the New World itself looked in Drake's time (nor exactly his tenuous relationship to the manuscript that bears his name) we can get a pretty good impression from it, reproduced in complete facsimile here for the first time.

For several reasons, *Histoire Naturelle des Indes* is a complicated document. The hands of at least two different scribes and two different artists are discernible, making it a figure of speech to allude, as I do, to a single author or artist. The manuscript is carefully divided by subject: sixty-two botanical illustrations come first, then some eighty-nine drawings of fish, animals, and birds, then forty-three drawings of Indian, Spanish, and slave activities. Four geographical views are also interspersed. Some drawings are well rendered, others mere daubs, but most have a kind of buoyantly piquant vision of their subjects. Some are true to life, some—particularly the fishes with doglike snouts and ears—arise from an almost medieval fancy, and some may reflect a knowledge of printed sources. But with two exceptions, all the drawings illustrate the Indies, and they name nearly thirty of Drake's regular ports of call. The geographical information in *Histoire Naturelle des Indes* constitutes the strongest link with Drake.

And the two exceptions? One is set in the Pacific; its text mentions Gilolo, an island in the Moluccas, which Drake visited on the circumnavigation. The other is set in "Loranbec," a mysteriously named province, which, says the caption, lies between Florida and Newfoundland at 36 ½ degrees latitude. Drake visited this part of the world, probably near present-day South Carolina, on his way to rescue the failing English colony at Roanoke in 1586. The captions to these two drawings mention Francis Drake by name.

Though we will almost certainly never know the identities of the "author" of this work, the manuscript does contain one extraordinary clue as to the kind of person or persons they were: the text. The French captions provide a sharp picture of the region, often more accurate than the drawings, and once they give us a glimpse of one of their authors. In the drawing on folio 111, an Indian tries to stop a European man from entering the night forest where a devil lurks behind a tree. The European is a self-portrait of the "author." Though the drawing is vague, the text is not so reticent. The Indian fears the devil and asks the author how he can be so bold as to walk abroad in the night. "I answered him," the caption reads, "that he must believe in the crucified Jesus Christ up above who would deliver him of all his diabolical visions if he firmly believes in him."

With its strong emphasis on the efficacy of faith, this statement indicates that the author was Protestant, most likely a Huguenot. Drake is known to have sailed with Frenchmen in his crew—Huguenots, almost certainly, because of his fierce anti-Catholicism.

All early visions of the New World have the power to haunt us. We search them for signs of innocence, for an Edenic imagining of a world we know too well, just as we continue to consult mirrors for lingering traces of our childhood. This trait is less a measure of nostalgia for a lost world, a time when several continents remained undiscovered, than it is a measure of faith that when Europeans first saw the New World they responded as we imagine ourselves responding—with esthetic joy and a sense of moral promise. We have the advantage of hindsight over those first voyagers from the Old World, and it does not necessarily make us realists.

If we interrogate *Histoire Naturelle des Indes* carefully, it will not give us quite the answers we expect when we daydream about Drake. Instead it will tell us some practical truths about the way he and his contemporaries regarded the Caribbean. Sixteenth-century Europeans were less interested in cultural innocence than we Americans are, who live so long after the fact of our own discovery. It is all too easy to forget that there are few things rarer than a voyage of exploration without commercial designs. Much as we would like to think that Drake came to Panama for the good view, he really came to Panama for nothing intrinsic in it, just for the gold that was passing through.

And that is partly what the Drake Manuscript tells us. In it we see not a virginal world awaiting the hand of Englishmen or Frenchmen, but a world already shaped and overlaid by two highly sophisticated cultures, one European, one Indian. And for the most part, we see not a pre-Columbian landscape meant to evoke an esthetic impression, but a world carefully articulated into its elements. The "history" of *Histoire Naturelle des Indes* is analytical in purpose. It separates plant from animal, ocean from earth, beast from man. Plants and animals here are not usually depicted in their natural settings, but are examined as species in isolation. If there is regard for beauty, it is mostly for the beauty of what is practical. Plants, for instance, are pictured in an empty foreground and discussed mainly as resources, not as components of a broader landscape. With a few exceptions—drawings of Cayman Island, bush dogs, and a jaguarundi—only man is allowed to dominate a landscape, and then often just to demonstrate the good he has made of nature. In that sense, *Histoire Naturelle des Indes* is an early exercise in economic geography, charting use and profit in the New World.

This is especially true when it comes to the Spanish. The author has paid careful attention to the workings of Spanish colonialism, particularly the mining, minting, and transportation of silver and gold. One can easily imagine the strategic uses of this information. Where it concerns mining, the tone of the Drake Manuscript almost resembles that of an early treatise in economics or engineering, tinctured perhaps by the slightest surprise at the breadth and complexity of the web the Spaniards have thrown over the region. Though they devised a cruel and exploitative system, they are portrayed without repugnance. Here are some scenes, taken from the Drake Manuscript's drawings and captions, of the Spanish empire at its work.

In Colombia, a country "rich in wheat, meat, fowl and plenty of gold," African slaves risk their lives mining emeralds. They usually end their days doing so because in the high mountains where emeralds "grow," "masses of stone fall on them . . . and they die miserably." Indians gather gold from the "falling rain," which forms cascading brooks whose water "is very nourishing for having passed through gold." In Veragua, a province between Costa Rica and Nombre de Dios, mining is more organized and, because of tropical storms, more dangerous. As they leave the mines, slaves wash gold in barrels, dry it over fires in iron bowls, and surrender it to their overseer as a "tribute." From the mines, gold is brought to the royal forge where it is smelted, formed into coins, and stamped with its carat value and the arms of the King of Spain to indicate that a royal tax of one-fifth its value has been paid.

The handling of silver merits more detail. A raised smelting furnace is heated with wood and charcoal, and air is supplied by an Indian who pumps two bellows. To the melting silver, the Spanish add dead dogs and "a stone called tuf," which remove the "bad quality of the silver." Then, the text continues, "one of the Indians pierces the furnace with an iron rod . . . and the silver flows into the proper clay molds forming plaques and silver bars." More highly refined silver is converted into "Reales" which are marked with a small cross and the royal arms of Spain. In Peru, where "silver grows deep in the soil like iron ore in France," Indian women carry it to the furnaces. Then it is carted down to the sea by "Peruvian sheep," or llamas, which this artist of the Drake Manuscript had plainly never seen, for he gives them long spiraling horns.

Off the island of La Marguerite ("the pearl") near the coast of Venezuela, we watch Africans dive for pearls with ropes and hoop-nets from a Spanish frigate, its mizzen set to keep it steady at anchor. An Indian courier prepares to cross a stream, his letter held in a split stick or a wax-sealed gourd to keep it dry. Boats float down the "recent-ly discovered" Chagres River—often visited by Drake—which flows into the Caribbean southwest of Nombre de Dios on the Isthmus of Panama. (It has since been dammed to form Gatun Lake, part of the Panama Canal.) The Spanish used the Chagres River to transport bulky goods, while bullion traveled overland. And at destination's end, where treasure embarked for Spain, ships ride in the "beautiful and spacious harbor" of Nombre de Dios, captured by Drake in 1573, into which the road from Panama descends between mountains that rise behind the town. Tents and store-houses crowd the water's edge, and a solitary orange tree, whose fruit the colonists deny themselves because of the "heavy" climate, flourishes near the point.

The second culture visible in the Drake Manuscript, and by far the more important, is that of America's aboriginal inhabitants, already distorted by the presence of the Spanish. The Indian tribes represented here have long been extinct and cannot be pre-cisely localized except where, as occasionally happens, the manuscript names their homes. If there is simple wonder anywhere in *Histoire Naturelle des Indes*, it is here in the Indian scenes that fill the last quarter of the volume. Even on the pages where they are not pictured, the presence of Indians suffuses the text.

A note of admiration creeps in whenever the author describes Indians. Those of Santa Marta, clad only in penis sheaths and carrying conical poison dispensers at their sides, "are handsome and strong men, artful in war." Those of Loranbec, per-haps the Cusabo Indians of South Carolina, "are extremely skilful in battle," so much so that in an incident recorded nowhere but in this manuscript they forced "the

English fighting under Sir Francis Drake in 1586" to weigh anchor and retreat. But the author does not merely admire their military prowess. Of those who live near Santa Fe, Colombia, he says, they "are good workers with great skill and intelligence . . . making beautiful cloth of fine wool with which the Spaniards dress and fit themselves out." Venezuelan Indians "fashion in gold relief several kinds of animals for their enjoyment, which is something unbelievable to us since they are taught only by nature . . . to do this." The women "swim like fish in the sea." In the end, the author throws his hands up in awe: "they are so skilled that one could not show them any work they could not do."

Roughly the first third of the Drake Manuscript is devoted to plants, and the captions explain how Indians cultivated and used them. As a botanist, the author of the Drake Manuscript is not very sophisticated, for he often fails to distinguish between indigenous plants and those introduced by Europeans. But he is acutely aware of the way Indians have woven tropical vegetation into their lives, and he has drawn on their lore as a primary source of information. He has given us a textbook on how to eat well, stay healthy, and garner profit while visiting the West Indies. Consider these examples, all taken from the captions.

Indians eat raw pineapple mixed with salt to ease stomach pains. They use tobacco for toothache and as an eye-wash, and they mix it with balsam to cure wounds caused by poisoned arrows. From their gardens, they harvest onions three times a year, which they eat "as we eat apples." Using an unidentified herb called "bregele," they soften iron by wrapping the metal in its leaf, covering it with earth, and throwing it in a fire. They make arrow poison from a mixture of centipede flesh, bleating-toad blood, and mensenille (*Hippomane mancinella*), a tree so poisonous "that if a person looks up at it, he will be blinded for three hours afterwards." They are expert arboriculturists, especially of palm trees, from which they ferment wine. They cut away enveloping foliage so the palm, exposed to the sun, will make more sap, and they build a fire around it to deter "the poisonous beasts." Then they pierce the tree "to its heart in order to make the wine gush out." The manuscript also shows Indians engaged in obtaining means of commerce: two from Trinidad and Nicaragua capture parrots, popular exports to Europe, and another harvests wheat, which is exchanged "for wine from the Canaries, linen, knives, hoops and other things they need."

The most striking image of Indian husbandry appears on folio 121. The caption merely states that the Indian sows several kinds of grain in his garden to make his family happy, but the drawing depicts a garden containing considerably more than "several kinds of grain." According to Alice Peeters, an ethnobotanist at the Musée Nationale d'Histoire Naturelle in Paris, this watercolor shows the plants most commonly grown together in tropical Amerindian gardens. Among them are a papaya tree (upper left), manioc (middle left), gourds (lower left), perhaps a pineapple plant (above the head), a row of maize (right), and two bean plants growing on poles (extreme right). There are also several unidentified plants in the picture, such as the bush between the Indian's legs. He himself, using a long dibble, sows seeds in a raised bed of soil, a technique associated with Mayans.

The final section of *Histoire Naturelle des Indes* represents the domestic life of Indians. This is the most interesting part of the manuscript, because these drawings express simple human curiosity. Nothing pictured in them could have profited a European, and yet no European could have resisted their charm. Women tend babies, bathe children, bring fish home from the sea, grind maize in wooden mortars. Men drive away a woman's labor pains by playing musical instruments as they march around the house where she gives birth. A dog leaps to their music and from the roof a pet monkey watches over the entrance. Other men tend barbecues, spin cotton, and weave fishing nets and hammocks. And unlike the rest of the manuscript, where each drawing and caption stands on its own, a continuous narrative of courtship begins to evolve, a story that alludes to earlier drawings and arches across several scenes, culminating in the Drake Manuscript's final tableau.

Courtship starts when a young man visits the house where his beloved and her parents live. He brings with him all he owns—canoe, money, arrows, fishnets—and to the father and daughter he says " 'Hai Hai,' which means 'How are you?' " He is not allowed to eat with them until the next day, when he has hunted and returns bearing meat. He "brings as much as possible to show that he works hard to provide well for himself, his wife and family." Then he dines with his fiancée and her parents in celebration of the engagement.

The wedding day comes. Seated on a stool in the shade and holding a Guyana-style club over his shoulder, the father of the bride gestures with his left hand as he demonstrates the virtues of the young couple. Both bride and groom have dressed magnificently in loincloths, with a bead necklace for the woman and ankle bracelets for the man. The groom holds a rabbit in his left hand, a symbol of his prowess as a hunter; the bride reveals her skill by grinding corn in a basin. The whole picture is one of fertility and abundance. Behind the bride grows a coconut tree and baskets of food stand all about. A large iron pot boils beside a fine grass house, where one of the young man's oars can be seen.

Satisfied, the father says to his daughter, "You need this young man. He will feed you well; you see that he brings a lot of good things for us to eat, he works hard at fishing as well as hunting, he plants, gathers fruit in the wood, and, in short, does everything needed to feed the whole house." The father then turns to the young man and expounds on his daughter's skill at baking bread and dressing meat. After all the proper testaments of value have been made, the two are wed. "When they are married," our author says, "her parents no longer want to work and customarily their children feed them."

Then, as if to give the narrative a slow dissolve, the author of the Drake Manuscript closes the scene by contemplating the community to which the couple will belong. "In each village there is only one tribe, and they do not permit others not from their tribe to live in this village. They choose the eldest among them to be called 'Cacique,' who is like a king and whom they obey in everything. And when their land no longer bears fruit or is tired of producing, they leave it and go to live in another place where they cultivate the land and where they know there is fresh water. Then after three or four years, they return to their first land where they settle down as they had done before."

Those are the final words of *Histoire Naturelle des Indes*. Is it only a modern reader who hears in them a touch of art, the sure sense of an ending? It is impossible to know. The Drake Manuscript is a casement "opening on the foam of perilous seas." We can peer into it, but we cannot see answers to all the questions it makes us ask.

# THE FACSIMILE

In creating the facsimile of Histoire Naturelle des Indes, we have remained completely faithful to the original in all respects but two. The folios of the original were bound, or rebound, in the late 18th century. Therefore it seemed unnecessary, and perhaps wrong, to simulate the binding in this volume. And three of the leaves (folios 92v–93, 93v–94, and 95v–96) were bound as fold-outs. For this edition they have been slightly reduced and reproduced as full pages or spreads, with borders which indicate their true proportions. And finally, the penciled folios at the bottom of each right hand page were added when the original was acquired by the Library. They have been retained for the purposes of following the translated texts in the back of this volume.

# HISTOIRE
## NATURELLE
## *DES INDES:*

### CONTENANT

Les Arbres, Plantes, Fruits, Animaux, Coquillages,
Reptiles, Insectes, Oyseaux, &c. qui se
trouvent dans les Indes ;

### REPRESENTÉS

*Par des Figures peintes en couleur naturelle ; comme aussi*
*les diférentes maniéres de vivre des* INDIENS ;

### SAVOIR:

La Chasse, la Pêche, &c.

### AVEC

Des Explications historiques.

## MS.

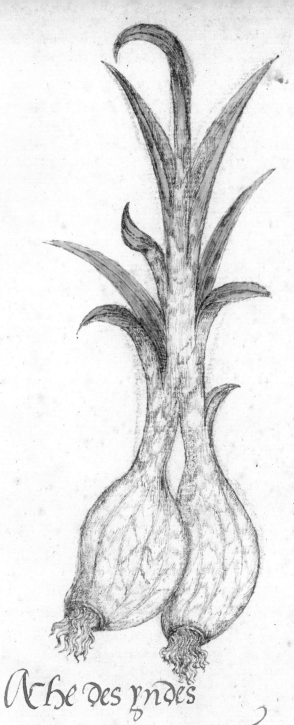

## Ache des Jndes

Jlz sont aulx qui sont doulx plus que ceulx de france
e sont ensemble e ne se departem point par fourche
Comme ceulx de france Les Jndiens en sont bien friam
ils Les cuisem au feu comme une poire ils Les mengem

## \* ANONNE \*

*Ce fruict se trouve au bois*

## \* ICAQVES \*

*fruict semblables aué prunes de Corsee.*
*Laissant le Carbme des Indiens et portent*
*noyaux aimé goust se fouué tendres*

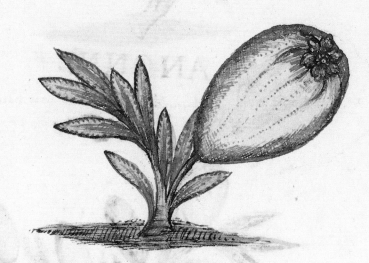

\* HAVOQATES \*

*Ce fruict ce trouue au bois*

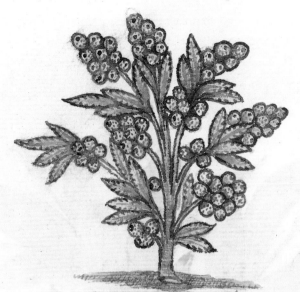

# HONNES

Raisin fort gros croissant au bois lequel
contient tel goust que la grappe de resin
duquel saide sa Indienne et en mengent dequoy ilz puissent
espardent le sont et luy buvent sans labter ne
somonent dhommes ames naturellement

# PINNES

fruict exquis et excellentement bon ayant goust de
framboise lequel croist en ung arbre hault ou il y en a plusres
ayant en nature de croistre plustost vers bas que en hault
chose contraire aux fruits dela france en mengeant ceux avec
du sel prennent peu oste le mal destomac aussi indienne

# PETVN

Herbe bien singuliere de laquelle usent les Indiens tant
pour nourriture comme pour medecine grandement profitable
estant malade hument la fumee par la bouche avec ung
chalumeau lors l'humeur peccante sort dehors par maniere de
vomissement souuent la puluerisent et la mettant a leur nez fait
distiller plusieurs eaux du cerueau pour le decharger Item elle
se treuue grandement secourable contre le mal des dens mettant
sa feuille sur les dens Roy par la douleur Item est profitable
pour alleger le mal des yeux et pourre Comment prendre de lag ...
et la mettre trempe dedans eau presque demy cart d'heure et
cy apres lauer ses yeux et Roy experimentera sa vertu

# *  AGOVQVES  *

Est une Racine dont usent les Indiens
pour faire du pain a manger et lappellent
cassaue laquelle mangée par Jaux auant que
Le soleil ait abune sur Raiona dessus Jaux sont en
Danger de mort Il puis lon comparaise aste
pagne ey une poisby Car le soleil par sa
vertu purifie Et oste Le danger

# *  PRENNELLES  *

fruict qui se trouue parmy le boid Et est
fort rare laiam une proprieté Dostir lastiraon
Des yndiens Et sons semblables aux prunes de
a pais de pruna portam aulleur or nagsst

# ✳ AGOVIAMME ✳

Il se produict par graines que sement les
Indiens ✳y leurs Jardins ✳ Ils viuent de ce
fruict ✳ Le faisont cuire ✳y leurs beaisses
ⓐⓕⓐⓜ ⓣⓡⓐⓛⓛⓔⓜ par le mengie des Indiens
Il dit uy grand nombre

·PETONNES·

Est ſing fruit qui croiſt dans les Jardins des
indes a vne terre nommée Caribara &
eſt ſing fruict fort bon et excellent quand
Il eſt meur Le faiſam cuire en La braiſe
Leur donnam grande nourriture

PETONIES

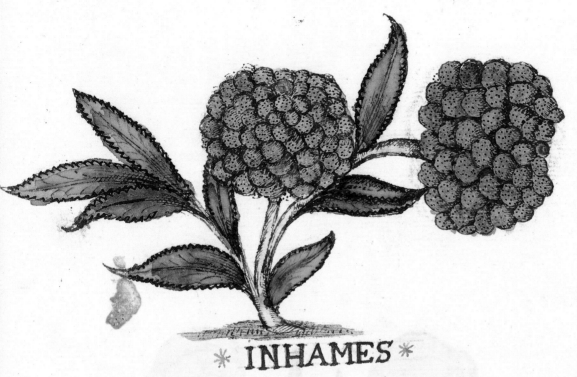

# ✳ INHAMES ✳

fruict excellent bon

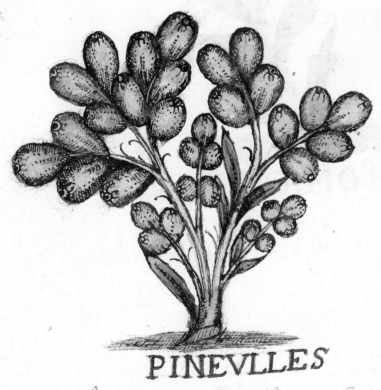

# PINEVLLES

fruict ayant goust de roisi duquel
sont très friandes contre l'altération

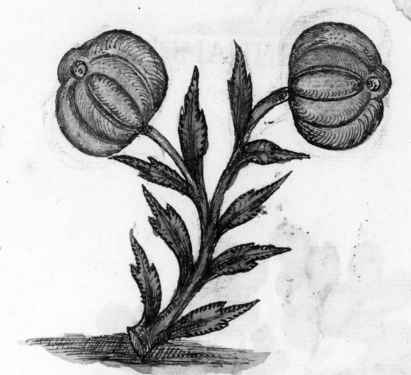

# * TOMATES *

fruict croissant au bois fort exquis
et se cuict auec poisson et ...

# *SIROVELES*

*fruict Bon an possible ayant*
*goust de Datte et croit en bois*

# *MAMEE*

*fruict Naissant au bois excellent*
*En bonté*

GOVNAVE

Le fruict se trouue dedans
le bois

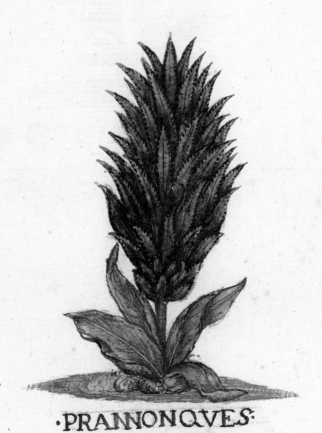

## ·PRANNONQVES·

Est Eng fruict qui Croist dans Les boix Excellem
Et de grande Substance Les yndes ostem Les fruilles
Dallentour Le polam Jusquea ce quilz trouuem
Le blanc du fruict puis Le mettem cuiril a la braize
Et Le mengem diam Le goust darbichault

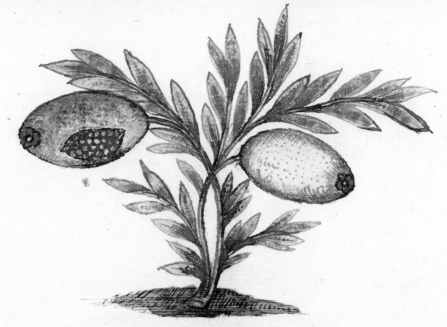

# ✳ GOVIAVES ✳

fruict grandement vtille contre le flux de sang
Estant mangé et Rsstrainct la personne
et estant meur a larbre est vng fruict fort excellent

# ✳ MAMONNE ✳

fruict Croissant au bois et fort excellent
a Manger qui est produit duy arbre aiant force
pointes aigue Dom a lentour de sa yndicuer ne le
Cocuillem ainsi Labastin auec vne gaulle aiant vne

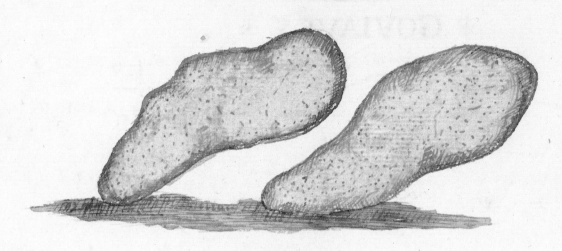

# ✳ PATATES ✳

De ce fruict vsent les Indiens comme dun
excellent manger & le cuisent auec viandes
en la marmitte ou a la braise La naissance
est de la terre sa figure comme vne rasine
& son accroissance vient par petitz morciaux —
Con appert que l'on plante ainsy & l'on faict vne graine
qui produit &c

# ✳ PIMENTE ✳

Il sapelle en langage Andoie hagut et en francoie poivre de brisil

## GOQUVES

fruict croissant en arbre comme Noix et estant la premiere
Couuerture ostraicte saparoissent deux yeulx et vne bouche
En faczon de poisson contenant dedans soy vng fort bon
Manger blanc en couleur mesmes aussy se trouue dedans la
coque vne eau bien exquise pour desalter de la personne qui soit en febure

# ✳ PLANTAINNES ✳

Son fruict semblable a la vigne quant vne
branche est compuee de cy reffette vne aultre
et est de la forme duy anambre long et est le
goust excallentem bon du treffora est bien deux de sa
menge cuist ou creu deelivy y en a en bien dispa—

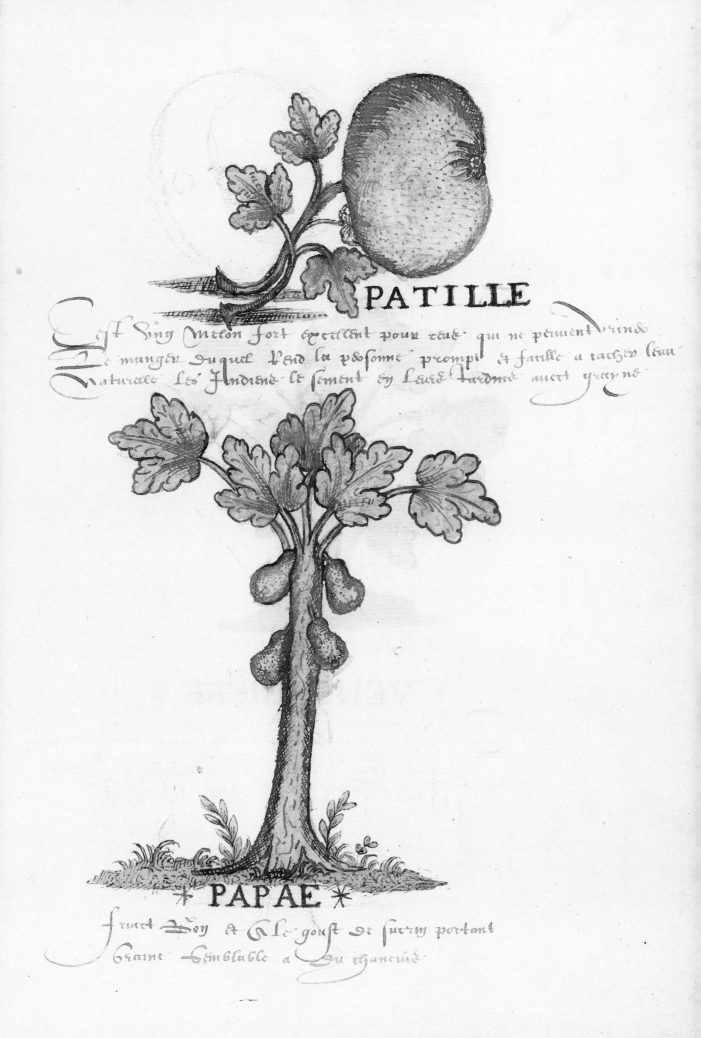

## PATILLE

Est ung melon fort excellent pour ceulx qui ne peuent rien
se manger duquel l'eau la personne prompt et facile a racher l'eau
naturelle les Indiens le sement en leurs iardins auec graine

## ✻ PAPAE ✻

fruict soy et de le goust de sucres portant
graine semblable a du thaneuie

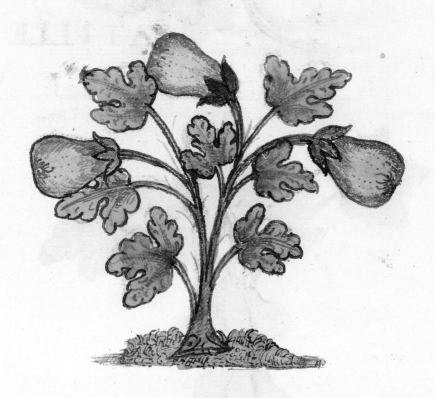

# ✳ VENRAGIERE ✳

Ce fruict croit de graines sucrees grandement
epiques pour chasser le mauuais sang de la
personne estant cuict auec la viande

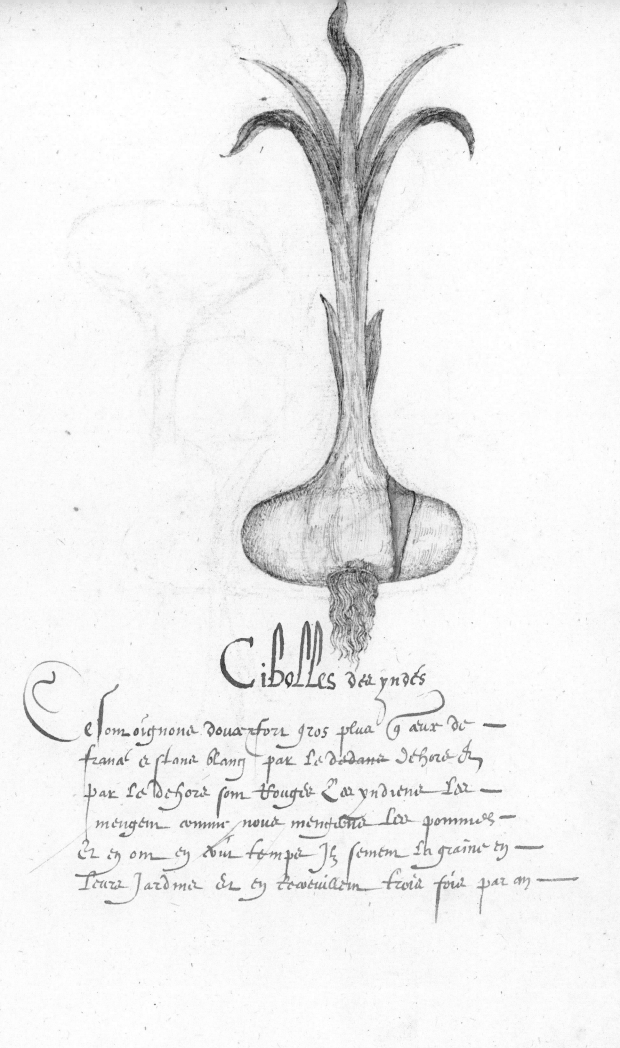

## Cibolles des yndes

Ce som oignons doua[r]fort gros plus g[r]aulx de
france et sont blancz par le dedans et hors et
par le dehors sont tousgie et les yndie[n]s les
mengent comme nous mengons les pommes
et en ont en toute tempes Ils sement la graine en
leurs Jardins et en recueillent trois fois par an

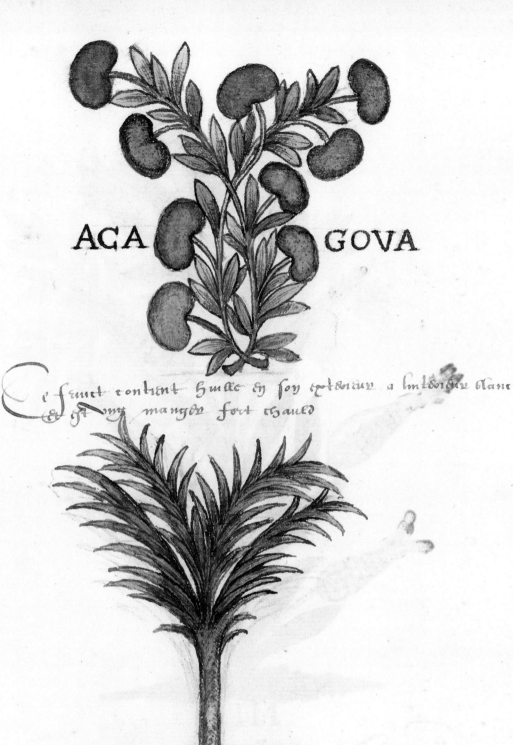

## ACA GOVA

Ce fruict contient huille en soy exterieur a linterieur blanc
et est ung manger fort chauld

## PALM ITES

Est ung arbre fort hault duquel lescorche
estant osté le manger est semblable aux choux
estant cuictz auec bonne viande

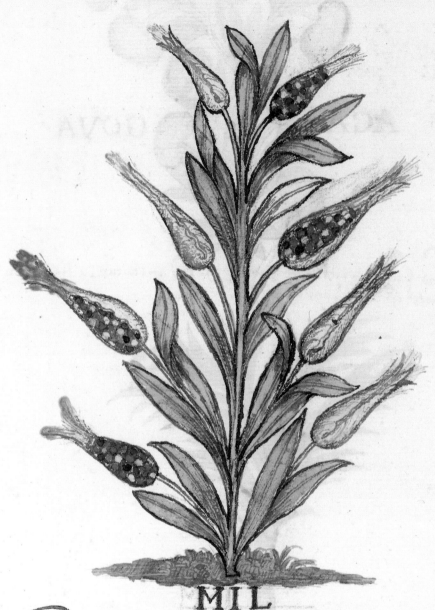

## MIL

C'est ung grain dequoy les Indiens vsent
pour faire pain apres auoir esmoulu dung
Moetier de bois alors c'est vne farine fort blanche
et tres bonne pour user de se moisonne
troys fois par an

BAL CE

C'est une gomme bien bonne pour guérir
les playes de sletches et aultres estant
appliquee auec du petun sot auffy
beaucoup pour guarantir du flux de
sang estant prinst auec ung oeuf

## FIGVE SAVVAGE

De ce fruict mangent Les Indiens
Ordinairement Se croist au bois

## ·TORCHALES·

Est ung arbre qui ne porte point de fruit ny de feuillar∼
il a forme pointu et est fort dur et beau par le dedans∼
il est madré ferram sur la culleur de violec aiant lodeur
fort bonne et Excellent

·TOPCHALES·

## GABOVCLE

Eſt arbre Croiſt au boiſ Lẽſ Jndiẽnſ ẽ
ſont Cordeſ et L'etz pouu pẽſcha poiſſonſ

## BREGELE

Ceste herbe Sett pour atendre le dur fer
Jls prennent la feuille auert de la terre
quilz appellent la barre et enueloppent
Le fer et ladicte feuille et le dorent de
Ceste terre et puis le Jettent au feu et
estant le fer eschauffe en telle farce
Jl deuient autant foible comme plomb

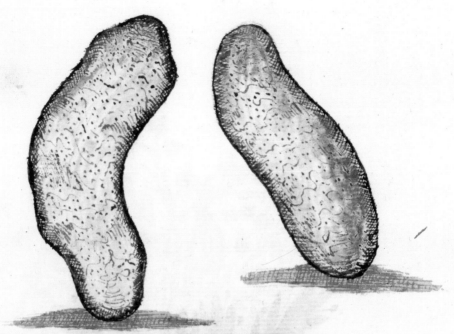

# ✴ PATATES ✴
### de la marguerite
Ce fruict aussy se mange au lieu de pain
apres auoir este cuict a la braise

# ✴ ROVMERRE ✴
herbe fort bonne contre l'air vicieux les Indiens La
gettent au feu en Leure maisons pour brusler & sil se
trouuent quelque bestes venimeuses ou de quelque espece
que se soit sentant la fumee de ceste herbe meurt
a l'Instant et par mesme moyen tout le venin s'absente

## ✳ CANBRE ✳

Cst arbre fait contre le flux de sang lon prend
La feuille oy la ville auert du fel et eau dont
Morties et puis la bouent a Linstant se trouuent garis

## ·FRIGOLLES·

Cest a dire fabuie aiana pareillon apres que le
fruit qui croist dans lesdites cosses est rond
Comme poix Zet yndes ses nourissem
et est ung monger fort bon Croissam dans
Les bois et les metem au feu et guand la
Cosse sent le feu elle souure et ses menssem
aiana le goust de marrons

## AVILANES · BLANCHES GOMITES

St Autam adirel Comme noir blanches Jlz ne
som point sy fortte ny corrosuere comme les noires
Contre lestomarlz ilz ne som point Lomir par
La bourhel

## AVILANES·NOIRES·GOMITES·

Est autam a dire comme noix en cest arbre croist une
Ispece de petites noix En en ya de deux sortes de noires
e blanches Quand une persone en a Mengé Il getem
tout ce quil a dans le corps par hault e bas/ Quand les
yndes sentem quilz ont Mengé ou quelque beste venimeux
La vuthel Ilz prengnent de ces noix promptement Jetant
tout le venin par la bouche e par bas et sont garantis/

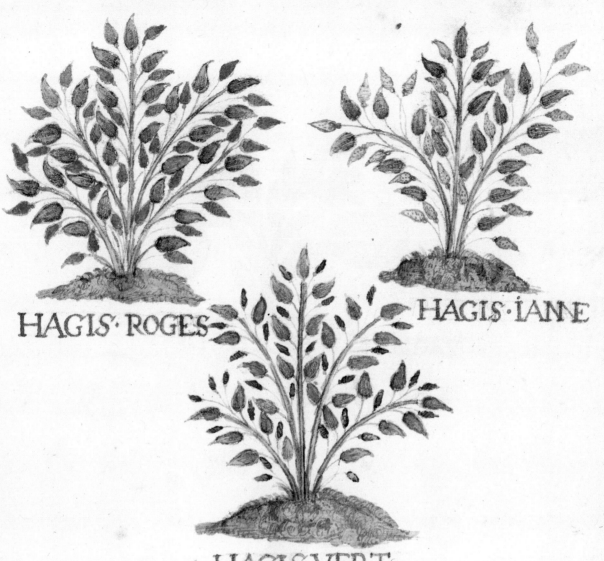

HAGIS·ROGES    HAGIS·IANE

HAGIS·VERT

Hagis vault autant adire en langue d'inde.
Comme poivre Et en y a de troir sortes
Mais le plus petit qui est le vert est le
plus fort et la feuille est fort bonne a
mettre au potage et en sallades Les inder
Briet a poivre auc du sel Et le mettem
dans la robbe de miel Et quand ilz vont sur le
pais loingtain ou ilz ne peuvent trouver d'eaue
douce pour boire Mengent le plus de ce poivre
quilz peuvent en cheminant et ne sont aucunement
Alterez estans tousjours frais Combien que la challeur
soit fort vollente et sont tous motz.

# * CHATANE DES INDES *

Ce fruict croist au long des eaux

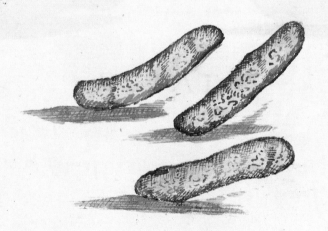

# * MENNIL *

Est vne racine qui croist a liste de la
Marguerite estant reullye Jls la mettent
seicher au soleil et puis sy vsent come du pain

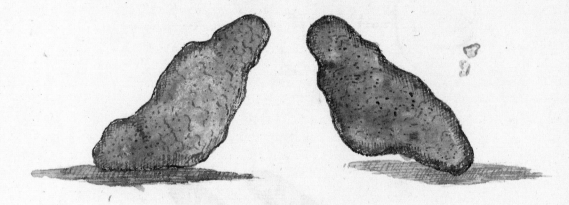

## * PATATES *

Les Indiens font de et ry briuages. Les ayant
faut Boullir audt eau et espramd dy lamain
Sen Juruent Comme du vin

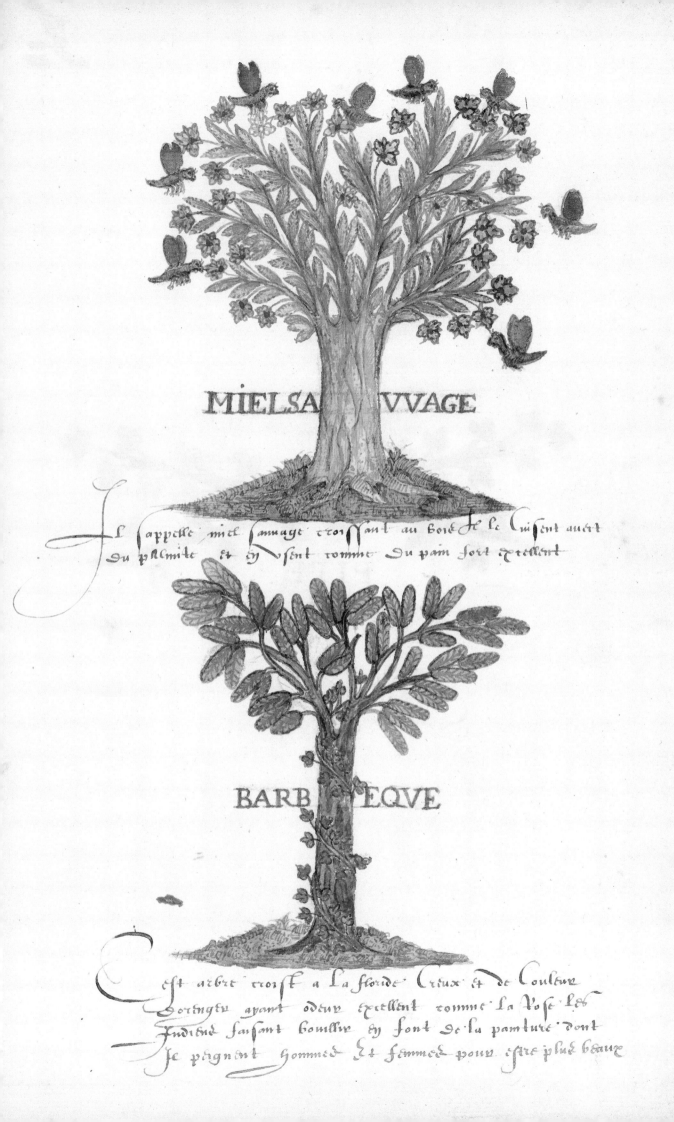

MIELSA[...]VVAGE

Il sappelle miel sauuage croissant au bois de le cuisent auec
du palmite et en vsent comme du pain fort excellent

BARB[...]EQVE

Cest arbre croist a la floride creux et de couleur
orengee ayant odeur excellent comme la rose les
Indiens faisant bouillir en font de la painture dont
Se paignant hommes et femmes pour estre plus beaux

# PİTE

est arbre croist au païs de lerayne
en la puide de la madalaine aultrement
appellee la grande puide fl en tirent
matide pour faire fil beau comme la soye
eyant couleur dargent

## ·MADAE·

Est ung Arbre qui ne porte nul fruict Il
est le plus beau bois quand Il est despouillé
qui se puisse voir et est entre les bois le
plus dur qui soy sauroit trouuer aians par
le dedans culleur de pourpre estans madré
beau par merveillens Il a lodeur bonne

## CARANE

est vne gomme grandement excellente
pour garantir de tout mal de roste
estant applique en fachon denplastre
sur le roste plus Dolent

## MENSENILLE

Arbre fort venimeux que se la personne le regarde
par hault de soba troys heures sans pouuoir veoir
par apres en cest arbre cachent leure flesches les
Indiens quant se vont en guerre pour les rendre venimeuses

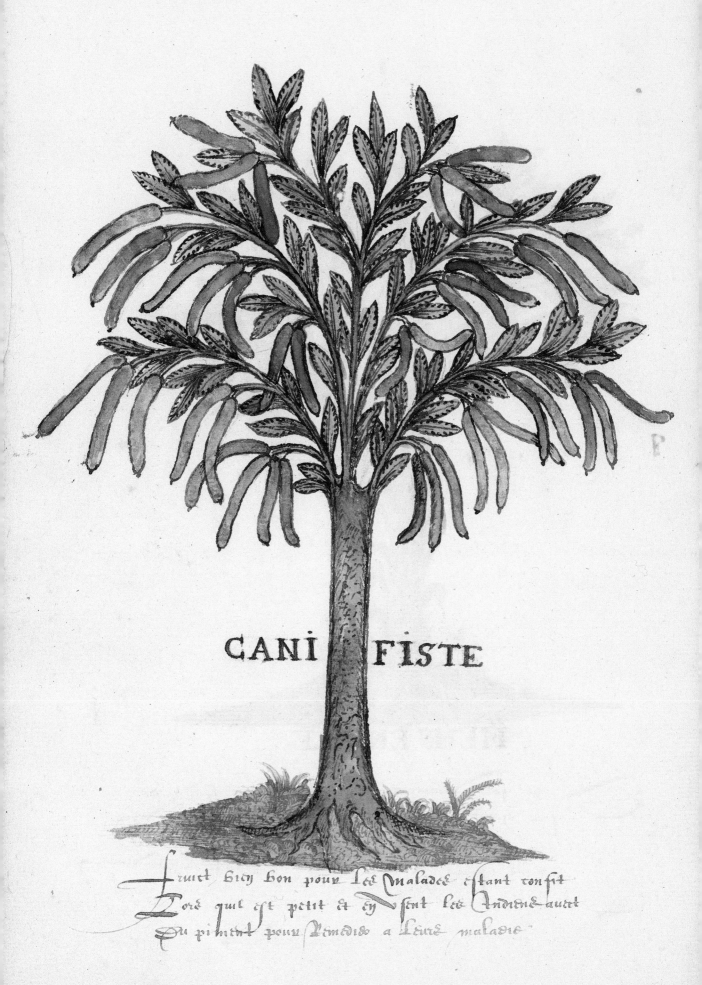

CANI FISTE

fruict bien bon pour les malades estant confit
Lord quil est petit et en sont les Indiens aussi
du piment pour remedier a leure maladie

# LACIQVE

Herbe bien propre a soulager ceux qui sont rpes par trauail
Estant bouillie auec eau loy sen frotte La plante des pieds
et Le font de la main pour prendre toute douleur

# SACA FRAS

Arbre croissant a La floride bien auant dedans le pays
Les Indiens en font du vin de la racine de la quelle
Racine se trouue bonne comme canelle et autant excellent
comme muscadelle et croit soupte le cap Sainct augustin

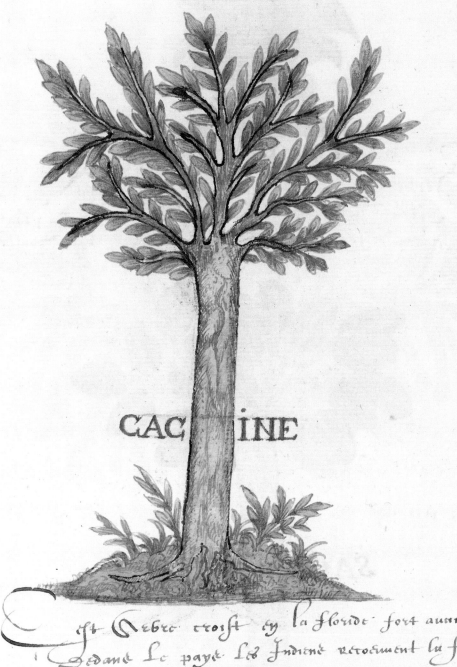

CAC HINE

Cest arbre croist en la floride fort auant
dedans le pays les Indiens recoeuuent la feuille
pour en faire breuage bien bon apres lauoir fait
bouillir auec de leau et la gardent vng an durant
et sen seruent de ce comme du vng

## Miatona

Æt vng arbre qui croist dedans leur cauee
Et porte vne graine noire fort Excellente
pour taindre en sou et coulleur noire Laquelle
Est fort belle Les yndiens en taignent ordinairem~t
leurs Accoustremens de Coton

## Chuppe

Est vng arbre qui croist au milom des bois —
et porte vng fruit fort Excellent Leu yndiene
no seut sadnanturir pour en aller quirir a raison
dea figura q dea couleurdea lequelles counternent
en trucin e en Meingena quand ley fruit est ûmbe'
en Abril

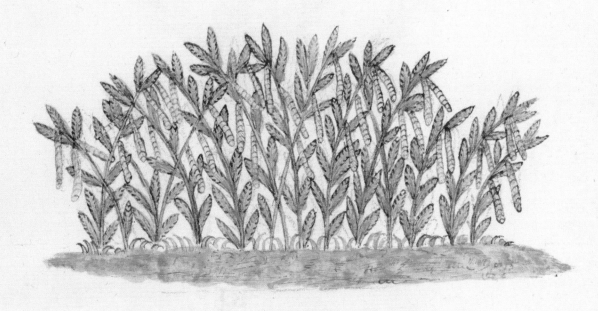

## COVCHEQVOV

C'est une espèce de grain qui est fort bon.
Et est au semblable au ris les yndiens.
En sement dedans leurs jardins ainsy comme
l'on seme le bled et s'en nourrissent en travaillant
deux fois par an

Comme le Coton croist aux arbres

En Cest arbre Croist le coton dans la
bois lez yndiens orfom leurs haie po teloire
leurs Jardins Et dedans le coton y a une petitt
grayne noire d'ou prouient le coton es y
prens acroyssement

PAL_ME

Arbre dequoy les Indiens tirent en contenant goust
Et platz Je couppent les arbres Dauprés portant umbrage
a ffin que le Soleil ne soit Byeffé Donorme plus viuement
a chaleur car dautant plus que le Soleil y est vif de
Dauantage larbre plus de Dit Je portent aussy ledit arbre Jusquau
au coeur pour faire saillir le Din mesme font grand feu aue
enuiron pour aruder les bestes Deminense

## PIAHOVNA

Est une espèc de mouelle ou coist du poisson
semblable d'oce congrece Et a la tesse d'une aulocruro
Et se trouue dans les tuuieres douces Et nest bon
a monges Nause quil est amer senfans La base
huilleux et douceurs

## SADRE

Sadre poison dee Indee

## BECVNE

Becune poison dee Indee

## SAVALLE

Savalle poisson bien gras et bon a menger

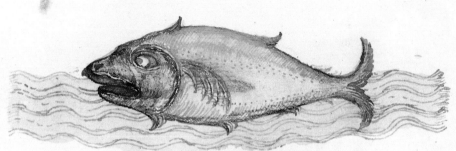

# ALEBACORE

Lebacore poisson dee Indee

# PATIN

Patin poisson dee Indee

# GRANT HORAIGE

Grand horaige poison des Indes.

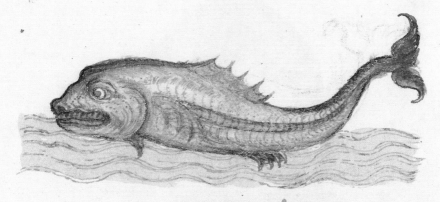

# DONSAILLE

Donsaille poison deau douce

# MORAINE

Moraine poison de perle sancte et
abitt fort dans les roches dans
la mer

# MERE

Mere poison faulne

## RES

Poisson des Indes qui a la peau fort dure
Ilz mangeit le fer comme une lime

## TIBERON

Ce poisson est fort malheureux a la mer
De fachon que sy ung marinier se jette
En l'eau pour quelque affaire ce poisson
Se tourne sur le dos et luy tire la jambe
ou le bras et le mange

## CAPPE

Ce poisson est dangereux a menger car
Con seul goust fait mourir les gens a linstant

## CHALIRATI

Ce poisson se trouue arme de pointe fort piquante
Sur le doz et directe se seruent les Indiens pour
mettre au bout de leurs fleches au lieu de fer

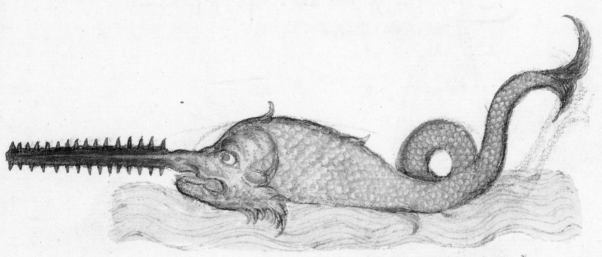

## PECHE ESPADE

Ceste beste marine est fort difficille a prendre
Et estant prins se rompt les pres auec soy
museau pour eschapper faisant par ce moyen passage
au aultres poissons prins auec luy

# ENCORNET

Ce poisson est fort bon a viscre. Ie se trouve
somet au Portzel

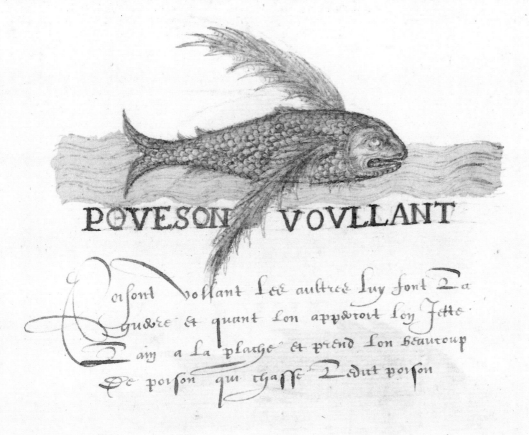

# POVESON VOVLLANT

Poisont vollant lee aultres luy font la
guerre et quant lon approit soy Jette
laiy a la plache et prend lon beaucoup
de poison qui chasse ledit poison

POISON VERT

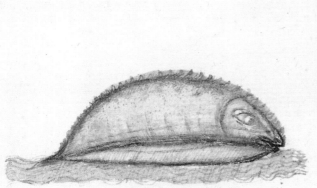

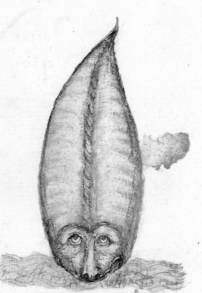

## CHAPIN          CHAPIN

Chapin poison bon a
Menger

## POISON VERT

Poison vert Le foye en est medicinal
Estant cuict auec patates Rouges
Leur guerir Leurs plaies estant flacges

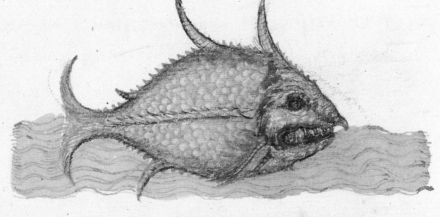

## LVNE

Lune poison des Indes.

## POVESONHERME

Poison armé qui Combat contre les aultres
par Lequel estant pique meurent a Inflant

## EGOVGE

Egouge poisson fort dangereux estant prins dedans
les rets se saulte et yeux des personnes

## SVRELE

*Surelle poison dcc Indes*

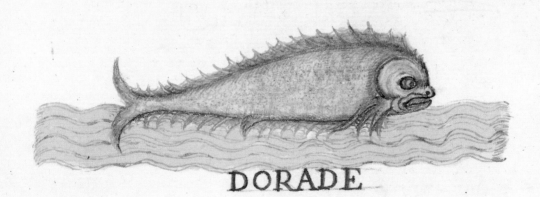

## DORADE

*Dorade poison beau et excellent a mengtr*

# BONNITE

Bonnite poison fieß bon au goust

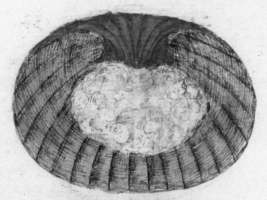

## CONCHE

Est autant a dire comme coquille si croist dans vne baie
qui est au bord dela Mer laqlle se nomme baillahoude si y affluent
riuieres douar le poisson qui croist dedans est derbon si deliquar
Lagll coquille est decouleur tuffe par le dossus si dedans est
decouleur biolecte

## CONCHE

Ceste coquille est belle si le dessus est fort tude Leau
indieux si en sucin pour grugr du Zingembre si du
mame qui est vne racyne dequoy ilz fom dela farine
qui leur sest enlieu de pain

# CANAV·DELAMERDVSVS

Ce Canau est de la mer du sud
D'une Jslle nommee gilolo en laquelle
fransisque drae engloix fit cettoise
son nauire pour parfaire son naviro
voyage de la mer du sud

## SETAQVE

Est vne pierre de couleur verte
qui croist parmy les lietz ou loy
pesche les palet scauoir dy La
margueritte elle somme comme voierre
et est fort excellente contre tout
mal de toste estant applicquee
sur Le costé dollent

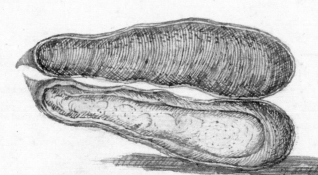

## HOVÎTRE DE LORANBEC

# CANAV·DANTIGOVA

De ce poisson se seruent les Indiens pour
prendre les aultres cest que premyerement Jl
apprinoissent Ꝗ le nourissent petit & quant Je
veullent pescher Je donne a mengeir a ce poisson
De la glandre de caiamant puis le gittent
dedans la mer estant amare dune ficelle
par la queue or les poissons sentant lodeur
De ceste glandre manges sapprochent de luy et
les Indiens tirent lentement la ficelle
pour faire approcher ce poisson ou cuaniro
Lequel est suyui par les aultres a linstant
gittent la rets & tout le poisson qui
suyuoit laultre se trouue prins

## GHVGET

Est vng poisson dur a vivre, en tans pluieux
l'on le faict boüillir c plus il endurcist
et estans hors de l'eaue habitue en terre ou
sur vng tillac de navire du dessoubz de sa gorge
il suce en telle sorte la terre ou le bois q[ue]
n'est possible de les th tirer que l'on ne le
face mourir

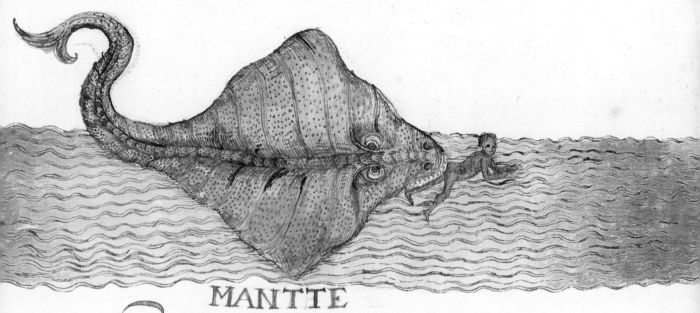

# MANTTE

Ce poisson est fort grand et moy moins
malicieux estant les naigeurs plongez
en la mer pour prendre les perles Jlz
se gettent sur eux pour les faire noyer
en apprés les mengent

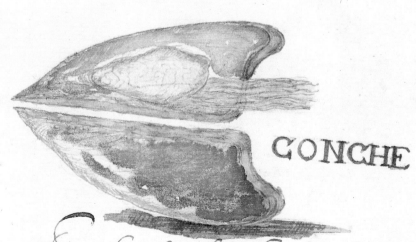

# CONCHE

Et croist la ou l'on pesche les perles dedans
ceste conche se trouue ung estang poil come cheueulx
de couleur d'or et est fort excellent pour persones qui
auroient mal en oreilles ou quilz seroient quelque peu
sourdz Jlsont serez au soleil et puis le mettent en l'heure
oreilles Jncontinent expediment sa vertu de se usant
souuent les naigeurs estant offencez en oreilles par
frequentz plongementz

# HIOGANE

Eſt vng ſerpent marin et tariẽ fort
dangereux auquel La morſure eſt Jncurable

# CHATILLE

Et poiſſon abite ẽ mer et eaue doulce ẽ
La tevre ſe lociubte entre la fonde et
tevre menfue et ne vault riẽ a mẽger

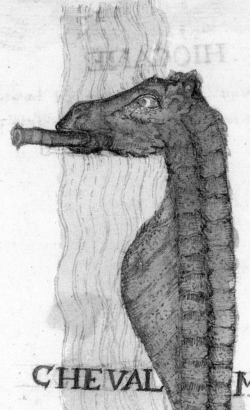

CHEVAL MARIN

Cefte Befte fe troune en l'ifle de la
Marguaritte ou on pefche les perlles

# HOMMAR

Il se trouve sedans la mer a une Isle appellee
les bastiments entre nombre de droit a la viuide
de sagre ayant couleur de violette et les come rouge

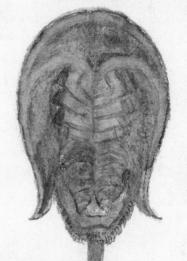

## LEDESVS

## LEDESOVS

## CAXQUENOC

Erable de la floride

# CARACOLLE

*Poisson de la floride*

CRATON·PORC·ESPIC·DE·MER·

Est vng poisson fort danglereux Les autres
poissons se cachent et fuient deluy et a.
Tout son corps couuert de poinctes Comme
Les plumes dun porc espic

·PATONNE·

Est ung poisson fort excellent a menger
ayant legoust dun esturgeon et habitent
souuent aux riuieres douces ɫ

# TORTVE ✳ NICOTE

*Ce poisson croit de bois proche de luenes*

# TORTVE

*D eau douce en la floride et le mange est fort excellent*

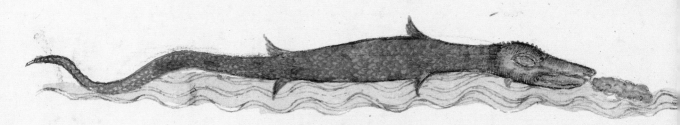

# VIVREE

Ceste beste habite es bois et vins des doulces
et fort venimeux se se seruent les indiens
pour empoisonner leur fleiches quant ils vont en guere

# TORTVE

Ce poisson a quatre piedz de long et deux et demy
de largeur lequel par le rapport des marinniers
peult vivre Jusques a cent cinquante ans Jese
trouve en l'isle de raiamant Je habite en la
mer et terre Je contient grand nombre doeufz le
mengeu en est fort bon

# CAIAMANT

Maim ce poisson est terestry et aquatique Jese
trouve entre la terre ferme et l'isle de raiamant
ou Je ny a abitation d'hommes seullement se
trouve grand nombre de ces poissons aulx grandes
fortues

# CAIAMANT

Ce Caiman ce poisson a abite les bordz de riuieres
doulces dedans la teste contient une piedre bien
singuliere pour personnes grauelleux et qui auroient
la piedre les Indiens mettent celle piedre au feu
Jusques a ce quelle soit toute rouge puis la
mettent pour estandre dedans la portion ou breuage
du grauelleux et le patient ayant beu cela les piedres
que ost soient se brisent dedans son corps et son
vrinette y boue Item Il a quatre glandres soubz
les aisselles Rendant une parfum fort excellent

# COVLLEVVRE·NOIRE

Ayant neuf ou dix pieds de long
elle sont bonne à manger

# RACELLE

Ceste Racine fait beaucoup au Indiens
estant picquez par Couleuvre mesme
aussy quant elle courent apprés Iceulx
Iedans les bois pour les picquer endomager
gestent et celle mesme Racine devant les
touleurent Incontinent se retirent arriere

# COVLLEVVRE·BLANCHE

fort venimeuse et dangereuse Racontrant
les bois les Indiens elle se Iettent contre
eux pour leur nuyre

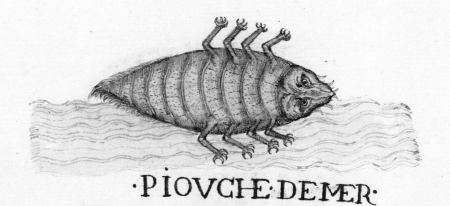

# ·PIOVCHE·DE·MER·

Ce vault autant comme poul

# ·ETOVELLE·DE·MER·

Ce poisson ne vault riens a mengd estant
fort venimeux sa retraicte tousiours
est au fauce sand cours

# PIRRAVGVE·DE·LA·MARGERITE

# PIRRAVGVE·DE·LATRENITE

Ces pirangues ont guerre mutuelle & istant
Lennemy prins & rendu captif tout le temps
De sa vie estant en guerre. Je en amour
Leur femmes lesquelles naigent autre la
Rame lors que leurs maris tomba estant

## CANAV·POVR·PECHER·LES·PERLES

Les perles se peschent en la mer entre la terre
ferme et la Marguaritte enuiron dix lieue a
troys ou quatre brasses deau par les naigres
lesquelz se plonge en la mer ayant en main
une truble pour descendre au fond ou estant grattent
la terre ou sont les huistres pour trouuer les
perles Et dautant quilz descendent plus bas en
leau Et de plus grosses perles trouuent et
ne peuent contenir leur alaine dauantaige que
ung cart dheure remonte hault Et rebut leur
truble la pescherie estant finee depuis le matin
jurquez au soir se retirent en la pescherie la ou
est leur domicille

Les perles se pesche en troys terre scauoir
en la Marguaritte en la Runde et la hatche
et au Cap de la vele

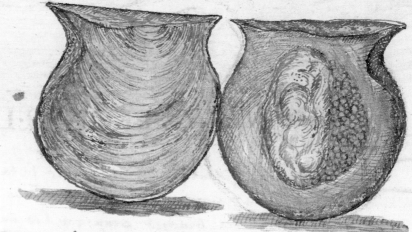

HOVITRE·HOVCROICE·LESPERLE

# CRAPAVLT·BELANT

Fort venimeux du sang duquel oult
La ceruelle les Indiens enpoisonnent
Leur flesches estant appliquee aultt
La feuille de la mancenille

# CENT·PIERNE

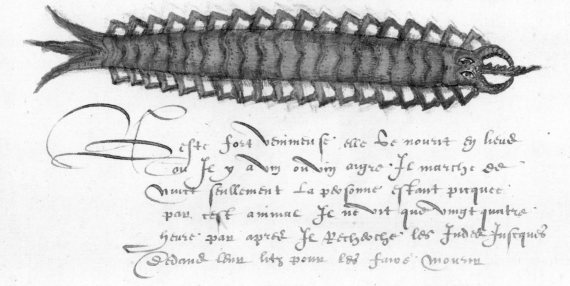

Ceste fort venimeuse elle se nourit sy lieud
ou se y a vin ou vin aygre Il marche de
nuict seullement La personne estant picquee
par cest animac Je ne vit que vingt quatre
heure par apres Je recherche les Indes Jusques
Oddand leur litz pour les faire mourir

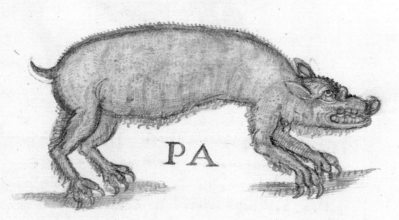

## PA

Ceste dont le mangier est grandement
Estime par les Indiens elle est de couleur
grise et blanche

## PORC · DE · MONTENNE

Ceste beste sappelle pourceau de montaigne
par ce que es montaignes abitte fort
Abille pour gripper se a ung nombre sur
le dos

# TIGRE

# FERMILLIERE

Ceste furieuse toute fois ceste petite beste
sappelle fermilliere lencontrant le tigre
Lors qune cherche sa proie et venu sant
fin. Le dos se tetent au col du tigre
Et luy perche la gorge autel le museau
et gued et ne le laisse Jusquee a ce que
soit mort a la place

## CABRITE SAVVAGE

Abitant ce bois est ung mengier fort excellent

## CIFRE

Est vne beste fort agille lesquelles ne sea peuuent apriuoiser ny nourrir
Car Jlz meurent de deuil et ne mengent aucunems depuis guilz som prins —
Jlz om la faac Comme vne personne & som fort mauuaisea et rigoureusea —
et se Jettem contre lea personnes principallemem A la faac de deuil /

## PATIA

Est vne beste qui habite dans lea bois elle a le corps Comme vne chieure Mais elle a
le corps fort long broutam comme vne chieure Cest vng excellem mengier laquelle —
nest facile a apriuoiser lesquellea en nourrissem en leurs maisons /

# MONTONS·DVPEROV

Ces montons seruent aux espaignes au lieu
de cheuaulx pour porter leur or et argent des
mines Jusques aux ville proches de la mer la
le mettent dedans nauires et le portent
en espaigne lors que la flotte des Indes
marche Je sont grands et forts Je heurtent contre
les personnes et les font cheoir par terre
Item Je montent fort bien les montaignes
du pays ce que ne scauroient faire les cheuaulx
et estant des dits montons paruenus es villes
ou Je tendent on les vent aux maistres des
nauires pour leur prouision ou a aultre marchantz

## Chappou

C'est ung chat saulvaige que se tient dans les boys.
Il est une beste mauvaise et fille et prompte à
monter à mont les arbres et fait la chasse aux
petittes bestes comme aux lieures lappins et
autres petittes bestes qui habitent dans les boys
et est le plus de sa nourriture.

## PERIQITE·LEGERE·

Le Naturel de ceste beste est de grimper
Le ventre en hault et grimpant ainsy va plus
fort que ne scauroit ung homme a pied la peau
de cest Animal est bien excellente au persones
quant ont le mal radur lon en romprent la
teste du malade puis rongnoit de quelle
graisse est ceste peau

## SAGOVAI

Cefte befte eft produicte au
pays de La payne

## CRABLE SAVVAGE

Ceft vne befte fort venimenfe et abite
proche des chruaulx et mullets et a vne
pomete a lextreme du mufeau de ce
puis quelle a pirque vng chrual ou vng
mullet Ilz meurent incontinent

## Perre Simarron

St autam a dire Comme chiens saunages lesquelz
som dans les bois et fom la chasse aux petits
pourceaux et aux veaux et les mengem ne vivans
Dautre chose que telz bestes et som ordinairem
dans les bois pour prendre leur nourriture
Les boeufs les vaches et pourceaux som leurs
petits dans les bois lesquelz chiens sonz dipaller
et apriuoisee estans furieux et Mauuais lesquelz ℔
loy ne puist Dompter sy loy ne les prend petits
ou sy loy ne les tuem

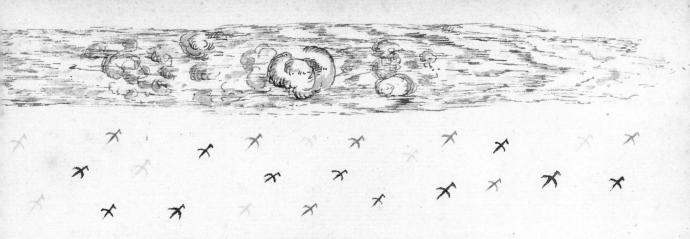

## ·VACHE·BRAVE·

Est vne vache fort saunage & furieuse &
estanz eschauffée Il ny a yndien qui en oje
approcher Ilz ne la peuuent dompter Elle
fault ordinairemenz sa demoure danz les bois auec
les bestes saunages laquelle beste est engendrée
dun thoreau & dune biche a cause q̃ les thoreaulx
sonz ordinairemenz danz les bois ou Ilz prennenz
leur pasture

# CHOVLECQVE

Est vne beste qui faict la guerre aux l'eurieu et
Connilz Comme faict vng Renard de ce païs Il a
deup conduitz Comme vne ciuette produisant vng
perfum fort excellen Lequel est semblable a
fien de mouton et la peau est fort bonne en
perfum et senteur

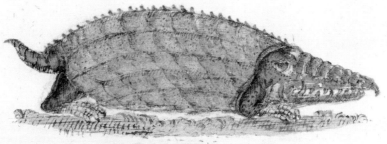

# CHVPA

Est vne beste qui se met dans la terre comme vng
blareau laquelle ne se nourrist que de fangues et nulle besti
nosiroit lassaillir Car Il retire sa teste et ser patte en vng
Mouceau dans son escaille laquelle est semblable a celle
dune tortue et est vne viande fort excellente a menger

# MONNE BARBVE

Celle beste est de la grandeur duy
Lievure quant elle voit les psonnes
et bois elle Rompt les branches des
arbres et puis les gettent apres les
hommes habitation de tes animaux
est ordinairement entre aux forestz
Dentre le Nombre dieu de panama

## · PORC · EPIC · SAVVAGE ·

## AGATILLE SAVVAGE

Cefte befte abitte a la floride et produict
beaucoup de parfum de muse elle a auffy
La peau fort belle tachee et couleure fane
Rouge de gris

## FLEQVE

Cest Anymae eft fort agille a grippe de
Arbres et industrie de tauac de fachon quelle
faict La guerre et Vimid et routre les poiffons

# TATOVAI

Cest Anymal se thασsε comme un
Lapind se vit de garine destest fort
Von a mangen

## ·AGOVTIA·

Cest Dang dest abitant d̃e Boik

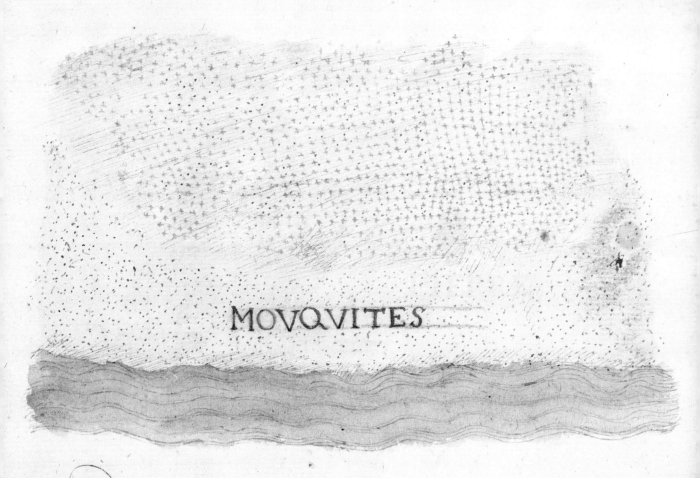

## MOVQVITES

Sont petites mouchez lesquelles som sy petites —
que loy ne les peult veoir elles som fort dangereuses.
Et quand Il ne faict aucun vent et que le temps.
est calme Ilz se meten en compaignies trouuans les.
personnes se gettent sur eulx les picquant en telle sorte.
que diriez que les personnes som ladres/la ou Ilz picquent
La chair senfle grosse Comme ung pois Et sy loy fue —
Lesdictes mouchez ou elles om picque les personnes —
elles les garantissen dela dicte enfleure Et en yndui —
som du feu en leurs maisons pour les estrangler
Et ne sapparoissem Que de nuict se tetiram
Le long du Jour proche dela mer dans le sable —

PIERRE

AIGLE

Des Indes cest oyseau contient en soy
Est nommac une pierre fort singuliere
pour les femmes qui sont en peine denfant
Et pour se souffrir de lad pierre convient
La mettre sur la cuisse gauche dilad
femme Et lors sera promptement delivree

# ·MARGANAHV·

Cy seau abitant de bois auquel
Le menger se trouve fort excellent

# POVLLE:DVPEROV

Cest oyseau prend sa retraicte en lieux fumeux ou lon
faict le feu et quand elle put entre es Jardins elle
menge les melons

## FLAMANT

*Oyseau bon a manger*

AVLTQVET

*Cest oyseau est fort huilleux se tieteage*
*comme Lapping*

## ·CEQQVAHONASO·

Cest oyseau a le bec plue grand
que le reste du corps

## ·PERDRIS·DES·INDES·

Ilz ont La couleur violette
Et qui est ung mengier fort excellent

76

## GRANT · GOSIER ·

Je ay le gosier plus grand que le
reste du corps contenant pres duy
ceau deau ou aultre liqueur Je abite
dedans les riuieres et mange les poissons
La grandeur est comme celle duy oyson

## · NOGALINAGE ·

Cette oyseau est semblable a ung corbeau Je vit
de charongne et meurt ordinairement de chalture de soy

## MOVCHE

Cet Indee est dune telle vertu donne
De nuict clairté sy grande que
facillement lon peult congnoistre
Lui presomee de deux ou troys espace
Et volle en l'air

## ·CATALI·

Oyseau de la mer du sud

## · GAGEAV ·

Est vng oiseau sauuaige qui fait la guerre contre les autres
oiseaux & est fort sauuaige Il habite dans les bois & quand
les yndes en ont prins de petitz Jamais ne les peuuent apriuoiser
Et estans courroucez se Jetent contre les personnes /

## PATÉ

Est vng oiseau qui habite dans les eaues douces & est vng fort bon Menger les yndes
les prengnent la nuit auec du feu Et voiant ledit feu y approchent Lesquelz yndes
leur font des apas auec des fiacres faictz comme lotz en prenant grand nombre

74

CASIQVE

Ceste fachon dhomme sappellent casique autant comme
Roy auquel Roy porte honneur & obeissance Et pour
estre Congnuz Jez ont vng enneau pendant au nez &
vng frontteau au front comme le voyes en figure Joe
aut landeau menduraut luy ny sar subgeez par lacoustume
quilz observent aucun poil sur le visage ny aux parties honteusez
hotes fueure seulement le poil du chevena de la teste quilz
laissent croistre long par lar longueur de lardeur du soleil

## ·HINDIANE·

Ceste femme chasse auōt vno clochette
pēndue a vne branche De feulle Los
mouchal De peur que pirquant Leure
enfand Jene pleuront ent voiant pleures
Leur enfand sont grandement fasches
estmant que poure Liord Le diable·
sort ĕj Leure Corps par visions estang
Leyf mouchal petetis piqus mouuicilon simon
Lay yndiena qui en prouioni enfleure grosse
omus poia Mais estang tuy allin stang ĕ fut
La piq quoure Je sont guarantis—

HINDE DE LA TRENITE

La fachon de prendre paroquetz est telle
quand le sont grands le font une attrappe
auec une roulte dedans ceste attrape mette
ong paroquet lie par les pieds auprés de luy
une petite beste appellee ratille qui le plume lord
le paroquet crie et les aultres paroquetz oyant sa
voix vienne au secours pour le defendre entrant
librement auec luy a la trape et que voyant ludicts
tire la roulte et incontinent les paroquetz sont attrapés

# ·HINDIANE·

Cefte femme pefche poiffon en mer pour
Nourriture de foy mary et enfant

# ·HINDES·DEIHONA·

Quand Cet Indict font maistre de leure
Enmemye Je les font toucher a terre puis
pillent Essiue apres leur donent ung coup
de leur espee sur la teste et commē Le sang
commence a sortir le trenc hatiuement estimant
par Le moydy Le Corps estre meilleur a Rostir
pour Le manger en grand Soumitte attribuant
cela a vaillantisse

# HINDIANE

Ceste femme bat le grain de mil
dedans ung mortier debois de bien
faire fort blanche dont font dupain
Ay boy de beaucoup nourissant

LA POISON

HINDE DE S·MATRE

Ces Indes sont beaux hommes et puissants subtilz en guerre
Entre Les aultres Indes de la terre de baillabonte se
assemble au combat Jusques au nombre de quatre vingtz
mille hommes et estant leurs enemys frapes de leurs flesses
vivent seullement vingt quatre heures par ce quelles sont
fort empoisonnes

87

HINDE · DE
NIQVE AVGE

Est y cy vne façoy de prendre peroquet
Ie ont vng matelad coffome par le bout
Et quand Loiseau est frappe Ine meurt
Mais seullement tombe estant estourdy

·HINDE· DE·
·GARIBARA·

Pour essaier si la poison est bonne
Ilz tirent sa fleches contre ung arbre
Et puis la retirent et quand la poison
Est bonne Larbre Laisse tomber ses
feuilles et puis meurt en momê de demy Jour
pour faire leur poison Ilz mettent ensemble
La feuille dun abre appellee menchenille
Le Sang dun Crapault blant auêc la
chair de cent pierre Le tout estant base
ensemblement le mettent dedans ung petit
pot de terre le couvrent diligenment
puis Le mettent dedans terre Lespace de
dix Jmes quivalle autant comme six moys
Et estant le temps passe Il essaient ainsi
que devise

## HINDE·DE·LORANBEC·

Cest Indes sont vestud et peaux grandement
habilled en guerre pour Leur forte ce que
peuent faulde Les england marchant en guerre
soubz le ⁶ francisque drac Lay mil ⁵ ⁴ᶜ ᵉᵗ ⁴ˣᴵ
sore aptentent prendre teste sore mais surent contraint
de souen les voilles et Leur veued pour la resistance
qui Leur sut saute La stitucion est entre la floride
et terre neusue par les 36 degmy de haulteur

Comē le bled croyt en vne prouince nommée le reste paÿs
des yndes du perou estant la dicte ona riuiere dans le pais
dou pro de bnē riuiere nommée la riuiere dela magdolaine
autres riuiere grande laqꝉe a sept lieuēs delarge ꝗ a fleuer
beaut donne dans la mer vnē grande lieue ꝑ dennie

Celle prouince est fertille en bledz chair vollarlle or ꝓ pierreries
Commes esmeraudes ꝓ autres pierres erquises ꝓ auoit ꝓ y auoit
grand nombre de cristal de roche beau brillant lesꝗ yndiens
ordinairemēꝉ en laꝗ prouince du bled deux fois par an lequel
Jls portent aux autres lieux ou Jl ny en a point dce moudre
par eux mesmes ꝓ mis dans des pourceaꝉ pour combler lenuoiant
par mer ꝓ par terre en xorque debꝉ dee canarie ville en france
Circler ꝓ aues chose qui leur sont nōsꝉsre comme ams a pescher poisson
pour nōꝉ auoie ꝓ deꝉ dee poisson

# HINDE·FLECHER·

Estant Les Indes fleuses a la mort oy Les
geslent sur une barbacoue puis La oy sont
ung fourneau ou ie y a ung canité qui va
rendre a la plaie du malade et alors que le
feu est alume ie mettent une feuille nommee
tabat auec une gomme qui sapelle balse et se
fort que la fumee entre ey la plaie du malade
prennent une feuille de tabat audt audt dela balse
dequoy faisant une emplastre Lappliquant sur
Le mal du patient est guaranty

## L'isle appellée fougue ou Isle de feu

Ceste Isle est de haulteur par l'estimation des naviguans de
troié a quatre lieues / Durant le jour l'on y voit au hault la fumée
de la fumée si grand le soleil est de sorte que la nuit est venue et
bien semblablement grand flambée de feu / a cause q dedans l'ysle
est au sommet d'icelle la terre porte souffre / et y voit on grand esclaire et
tonnerre qui cause les feu continuel / Et est l'ay Isle scituée dans la mer de
lune du nombre des Isle du cap verd lieu longtain de la terre ferme de dix
lieues ou environ / au bas le long de l'ay Isle s'y trouvent grand nombre de
pierre de ponce flotant sur la mer en laquelle habitent peu de gens

a cause que le lieu est desert et peu fertille / dauantage lad Isle
est dangereuse pour les nauiguans craignans approche dicelle
plus de deux lieues loing a raison quil la mer est fort haultte /

Ceste Isle est scituee dans la mer et est l'une des Isles de la
terre ferme du perou et la elle ny habitent aucune personne a cause quil ny a
point d'eaue douce haussy que la terre nest fertille en aucuns biens
sinon quil y en grand nombre de cayemans et tortues qui sont en la mer
et en la terre lesquelz estans prestz de faire leurs petitz gettent
leurs oeufz par la gueulle a cause que nature ne leur a donné pertuis par
le derriere et si sur le sable proche dla mer ayans esté proprieté
de les couurir aulx leurs passer dus sable pour les ainsi que
en le soleil donant a donné la chaleur dessus et formem des
petitz caiamans qui sont fort nauissans dangereux tant en
la mer et en la terre aumoins dequoy les hommes craignent a nouer
et nager dans la mer a cause diceux car depuis quilz tiennent l'homme
il ne puist eschapper quil ne soit traine et mengie la chair duquel
caiaman ne vault riens a mengier estant fade et douloureux au contraire la chair dela tortue est bonne la mengeoir laquelle a telle proprieté
que quand elle veult faire ses petitz gettent par derriere ses oeufz sur le

cayman

sable de la mer en grand abondance lesquelz sont jaune comme le rouge sl
loeuf d'une poulle tendz comme est loeuf, et son sans escalle naiant
q dela guelotte blanche a lentour ilz couvrent ses oeufz du sable dela mer
comme le caiaman et alora q le soleil donne dessua se forment et
petites tortues qui est ung daicellem mehnere Melmer les oeufz qui
produisent, qui ont tel goust que aufz de poulles Au surplus grandes
espacieuses aiant lestalle dure et espesse et voullans prendre
Jaeces commion seullement les vernes sur le doz lesquelz y estans
ne se peuuent plus tenmer et de ce sen prend grand nombre
a lentour delaquelle Isle y croist et se produit grand nombre
desponges propres ase lauer

## ·LA MANIERE· Comme les yndiens

vont a la chasse pour prendre les Lappins

Font vng enclos de haies comme des claies
Quilz nomment en leur langaige barbacane
Couppant lherbe ou les Lappins se tiennent
Retirez Et regardent deguel coste est le
vent y mettant le feu lequel sentant
fuient Estans au bout deladicte haie
Les yndiens sont les atendans et les tuent
a coups de baston

## ·COMME·LES·YNDES·

font la Chasse au poisson

Les yndes allans au bort dela Mer soiant Le
poisson se Jouée dessus leaue promptemens
Le flechons le faisans mourir Car estans
frappé Il ne peult plus nager ny aller
au fons deleaue

Le port appellé le nombre de dieu

Ce port est ung beau havre e spacieux tirant sept a huit brasses deau
auquel arrivent les flottes des navires despaignol pour faire marchandise
avec ceux du pirou estant scituée en ung lieu montaigneux de duquel
lair est fort gros et malsain ny pouvant durer long temps les espaignos

pour raison de ce pour n'estre habituez e accoustumez a l'aire du —
pais En sorte qu'ilz viennent le Iour espaignolz se gardent de boire eu —
seant l'eaue et de menger orenger a cause du febvere chauldde qui y
sont ordinaires Auquel pour arriuent l'or e l'argent du perou
pour traictee marchandisee auec Les espaignolz baillant or et
et aultre monnoiez en eschange pour marchandise Ilz craignent faire
venir les or e argent de panama par terre qui est en la mer
du sur distant Duy nombre dieu de dix huict lieues a raison
Des naigres simarrons qui robbent et pillent tout ce qu'ilz trouvent
par le chemin apparenant aux espaignolz Lesquelz naigres
simarrons s'assemblent par trouppes de peur d'estre surpris par
espaignolz Ilz viennent et Lors trafiquant Venans de panama
en ung nombre dieu passent troiz riuieres Eaue doulce ayant de l'eaue
Iusques a la moictie du corps Estans en grand danger quand les
eaux sont haultes Et sont ordinairement submergez en l'eaue
hommes Et mulletz portant marchandisee tant or et argent monnoie

Comé les esmerauldes croissent & se recouurent
aux montaignes

Lapierre exquise dicte esmeraude croist aux Montaignes fort hauttes
Et ont les esclaues naigres grand paine & trauail pour les avoir


98

a raison dela hauteur des montaignes es y finissent leurs journées
ordinairement et au soir en fouissant dans leurs rochers et surpris
pierreux les masses de pierre tombent sur eux qui les enveloppent
dessoubz et meurent miserablement Il se trouvent avec
Icelles grand nombre de cristal de roche beau et en grandes
pierres avec de listarge dor en abondance Lesquelles montaignes
sont dans une province nommée le raygne proche dune ville
nommée saincte foy Capitalle de lad province Qui est bien païs
Abondant en bledz et en volailles et grand nombre dor Les
yndiens de ce païs sont de grand travail avec grand experience
Desprit Ouurants et faisant de beaux draps delaine fine
Dont les espaignolz se vestent et saccommodent les faisant
taindre de diuerses coulleurs.

Come les yndiens cherchent lor proadam des Montaignes
par lore quil y a Inondation deauex bonance du ciel

Les Montaignes dicelux paux som fors hautes estimees
en hauteur par leir naviguance Iusques au sommer dicelle
Bonhommes bien Iusques a quatre ou cinq lieux de
haulx In sorte q lor est lauex dans naissure en qyndiens
ny peuuens montir a raison de froideux dicelle q froidure

Ausquelles y a grand nombre dor au hault d'icelles
lequel se trouve qu'il donne par l'affluance des
pluies laquelle forme des petits ruisseaux qui amenent
de hault grand nombre dor par petitz grains. Que
les y d'icelluy travaillent au bas des montaignes avec
des petites escuelles comme donne ouy cy dessus qui
est une grande richesse d'icelluy dit. Ou de a l'
les eaux qui en descendent sont fort excellentes bonnes
a boire et ne sauroient porter dommage a la personne
ains de grande nourriture pour en passe par l'or
avec et une propriete que qui oncque en boit Il devient
promptement et se descharge les rains de gravelle et
autres choses

Come les esclaues naigres trauaillent et cherchent lor aux
mynes en la terre nommée Perauquel

Ceste terre est fort dangereuse les naigres y uiuent peu de temps et ne
se passent Jour et nuict qui ne pleuuent auec grands esclairs et tonnerre
a cause q́ ladite terre est proche de la ligne esquinoctialle estant peu
fertille en blee Mais y a grand nombre de bon or Et le roy despaigne
permet aux espaignols qui sont aux yndes de sy habituer p̄ faire
mines et auoir lor estant en ladite en luy paians la cinquéme partie
de tribus de tous ses deniers tans dor argent que pierrerie

Et ne contraignent ny veullent permettre les espaignols que les yndiens
travaillent ausd mines de cram de guils naient la cognoissance dela
valleur delor Car silz cognoissoient leur feroient la guerre et les
chasseroient du pais lesquelz espaignols achaptent grand nombre de
naigres de laffricque pour leur fuir deselaves Et aiant
lesd naigres fini ^achevé^ la journee de travailler au
nombre de huict ou dix personnes En la sortie desdes mynes
y a une demie pipe plaine deaul ou ilz lavent lor appres ce
le mettent dans une escuelle de fer mettant icelle sur le
feu pour le seicher Et estant seiche lor lung iceluy au Maistre
dhomme guillas pelle mr dhostil pour vebr et sauoir par le
poix le nombre quil y en a Auquel maistre som subgch luy
baillet par forme de tribut la valleur delor reuenant au poix de
trois ducatz pour chacun jour Et sil advient quilz ne donnent
durant led jour la pesanteur dor desdictz trois ducatz sont subgch
neanmoins bailler led tribut aud Maistre dhomme En seducnant
quilz en trouverent plus grand nombre Iceulx feroient a leur profit

Come les yndiens cherchent lor en la terre ferme &a
yndee nommée borborat.

En Ceste terre y croist aussy grand nombre dor & ne permettent
les yndiens aux espaignols de sy habituer lesquelz sont experts
en guerre estans lor de bas prix & quand les yndiens sont
traffic avec lessy espaignolz bailleur dusor troia on ar pour une
tesglier ne valleurz que une on ar dor au prix de vingt deux carratz
dauantage lessy Indiens Comme estans Ingenieux font & esleuent
en bosse dus or plusieurs sortes dammaux pour leur plaisir
chose a nous Indroiable pour nauoir estet Instruitz sinon q
de nature qui les a Induitz à le faire

La forge royalle ⁊ ordinaire ou se fond lor prouenant
Des mynes, érigée par le Roy despaigne, afin deleuer
ses tributz

Il nest permis ny loisible a quelque personne que ce soit tant
nauchier espaignol que yndiena dauoir forges ny fourneaulx pour
fondre lor venam des mynes ch sone subtetz dapporter fondre
Jcelluy alaq fonte royalle pour en estre paie le tribut au
Roy despaigne qui se montent au cinquiesme de cutt chacuns pour
les tribut le Mahtre dhomme appellé mdt dhostel qui teau
salury tribut Marque lor des armes ⁊ armes du Roy despaigne
pour monstrer le paiement du tribut quils en ont fait de_
outre appose dessus aquelle valleur est lel or quand lessay
en est fait sauoir sil est de vingt vingt ung ou vingt deux
Caratz ⁊ffin ⁊ par ce par sonne sauchem le prix aquoy Jl est

Et sil est trouue quil naue la marque royalle du Roy
despaigne ny par les tresor lor est confisque & xulx
au fuix chosas comme argent pierreries & perles nauans par
les tresor Ils doibuent au prealable que passee doit
yndes en espaigne faire enregistrer a la contrestation
Le nombre delor argent pierreries & perles quilz enleuent
du pais /

Le fourneau ordonné pour la fonte de l'argent
venant des mynes.

Iceluy fourneau est hault esleué et estant eschauffé
par le grand nombre de bois et charbon qui y est mis prengnent
les Jndiens deux souflets et auec grand fort souflent pour
fondre chault les fourneau mettant l'argent dedans lequel
estant fondu et pour adoucir Jceluy gettent dans les
fourneau une pierre nommée fuf de couleur Jaune lacelle est
bien claire et a telle proprietté en soy d'adoucir l'argent et
ou se on tyene auter charongnar mortes quilz mettent
dans les fourneau et pour la grand puanteur des charongnes
et uertu de la pierre ostent la mauuaise quelle et giua —

Les argent le rendant doulx Mesmes estant jceluy fondu
y a ung yndien lequel auec une verge de fer peraem les fourneaux
par ung pertuis rond qui est au bas djceluy et allors largent
coullent dans des moulles de terre propres pour cest effet pour
moulle plaques et barres dargent Item est jceluy affiné
qui se rend plus doulx dont de là jlz en font des realles
monnoie du perou aiant d'Impression une petite croix et
armes du roy despaigne et de ce trafiquent ordinairement
et naiant argent monnoie baillent le poix dargent et
doit valloir pour deux monnoies le tout de grand revenu
et valleur au Roy despaigne.

Come les yndiens trauaillent aux mines dargent
en la terre du perou

Largent croyst bas dans la terre comme la myne de fer en ce pais.
De France les yndiens en trouuent grande quantité trauaillant aux
mynes au nombre de huit adix personnes par chacun Jour il sont
les mines assy dedans le pais proche dune ville nommée Limea
qui est la capitalle du perou Lequel argent est fort aigre venant
dela myne de roy esty tenant nature destaim et cuiure Mais
Largent qui procedent des mines des neufues espaignes est plus
venant dela terre meilleur que celuy du perou Ils apportent les
femmes desdi Indiens Largent des mines au fourneau pour fondre
et laffiner

## La Riuiere de chagre

Ceste Riuiere a esté nouuellem[ent] descouuerte par les espaignolz l'aguelle leur
sert a nauiguer leur petit l'or [et] l'argent venant du port de panama distant
dud[it] panama au cap[e] de croiz de trois lieues par terre [et] est le
commencem[ent] de ladite Riuiere et lors que la flote des nauires du peron est
arriuée au port de panama chargez comme dessus d'or [et] argent incontin[ent] ilz
portent led[it] or [et] argent sur des mulles par terre Jusques aux port
d'croix pour estre porté dans les barques par ladite Riuiere Jusques
aux nombre de dix[e] ch[e] par ce moien sont hors du danger d'y nauiguer
marronne appelez uulgairem[ent] bolleura Jusques le quel port d'croix
Jusques a l'ent[rée] de la mer qui est la fin de laste Riuiere de chagre

Distant luy del'autre Biron neuf lieuües Leur barques ne tardent
aucunem adeuallir en la mer pour sacheminer auf nombre dieu
a raison du grand courant deladite Riuiere lesquelles barques
sont toutes chargees d'or d'argent ny aiant d'autre hommes que huict a
dix naigres esclaues pour nagir quand ils nom son propre
ung espaignol seullement appelle le mahieu d'homme qui leur
commande / Ce faict estant arriuee auf nombre dieu descharge
faict du sor d'argent portent marchandises propres pour
portee auf panama / dela au pirou Estant contraints descharger
moitié de leure marchandises a lagrange lieu proche deladitte
Riuiere de chagre Cause que les barques ne peuuent monter
laf Riuiere sy ne sont allees pour raison de l'impetueux courant desden
diuelle et a laste fin son contraints de poussee auec perchee lesdictes
barques desorte que pour deualler laf Riuiere chargee de tresgrande supplie
Il ne leur fault que le temps de spase de six a sept heures
Et au contraire a temontee Il leur conuient auoir auffy quat
cing Jours de temps /

Come les femmes yndiennes sont en paine
d'enffans

Les yndiennes estans en travail d'enffans, les yndar=
s'assemblent auec leurs Jnstrumens et son bon a l'entour
de la maison qui l'appelle la bouchie en danssans faisans le plus
grand bruit quils peuuent Chantens a haulte voix disans to=
par tel moyen la douleur de ladicte femme se passe

Come lay ndienc feuicmem del a carbouti au frem dit
Lebois

Les yndiens venant de la chasse apportent pour estre
sauuaiges pour la nourriture deleur femmes quand
ilz sont delinre delturé enffant Il fana gra to ele
viandt est la plus excellente des nourrissante qui
sont aux yndes

Comme les yndens bouquant ou rotissem le poisson
& la chaïr

Les yndiens font dvny grand feu de borans & le bois est consomé en
charbon prengnem quatre fourchettes debois e les fichem en terre de mesme
plus a bafone deschauere dossus lors pour eschter de hauteur du feu dony
pied e demy en apres a estendem leur poisson e chairs quand il sont
la chaleur du feu la fumet de la graisse qui tombe dans le feu fait
bouxanie ou rotir lay chaïr e poisson & est vng bon mengier e le
vurnt souuem en peur quil ne bruste en ostam lay chaïr e poisson
cuide betur a la couleur de charbon for

Come les yndienmes dont leurs leurs enfans a la mer
quand il est la plaine Lune /

Les yndienmes menem leurs enffans a la mer de
leu lauter la mere en tiens ung par la main
de lautre se mett sur son dos et leu netouent bien
de facon quils nom aucune galle ny tongnes
desors noh par eux le corps ed nagens leh
yndienmes Comme poisson a la mer

Come les yndiens ont ordinairem̄t des Illusions
du Maling espirt

Les yndiens sont fort tourmentés la nuict par visions du
maling espirt qu'il appelle en leur langue athoua et
ne se sortir de leurs maisons durant la nuict
et le jour ne soit venu en ce leur proviem acause qu'ilz
n'ont nulle croiance ny enseignement de n'adorent chose
quel conquer Comme peuvent faire les nations de
barbarie quinte ny du bresil En estant ung jour ouché
en la maison d'un yndien et sortant d'icelle de nuict fust qu'il

par les Juifz de mᵉ retiree en sa maison me —
disans quil debvit attour a quil vault autant comme —
le diable Me demandans le lendemain matin loccasion
que Je navoie aucune peur &c qui causoit ma hardiesse
Alors luy feiz responce quil falloit quil eust creance
A Jesus christ crucifie qui est lahault &c celuy la —
Je demeroie de autre superstition diabolicque &c
aviant fermeme en luy Ce que entendans me dit que luy
La que estoit la hault nestoit bon &c nennoioit que
du froid pluie &c soleil qui soit traison Mais que celuy ·
qui estoit en terre &c baile leur estoit bon &c leur donne
Journellem nourriture Comme pain · œufz chair poisson ·
fruitz &c autres biens procedans de la terre Mesmes que
leur quilz mouroient Ilz y estoient enterrez A quoy feiz
responce que dieu seul createur avoit cree le ciel &c
La terre &c que par luy du riens chosen ont este faictes
&c estoit celuy mesme qui arrouse la terre &c le chauffe
qui fait sortir les fruitz desquelz grace Ihom leur
nourriture —

## Comme La Vigne Croist aux yndes

Les yndiens plantent La vigne en façoy de tribille
et ne leur est permis dey plantes qu'en leurs Jardins
et non ailleurs Aussy nest permis aux espaignols ny
yndiens dey plantes en abondance ny d'olliviers
pareillem~ attendu le grand tribut que la roy d'espaigne
prend sur al Enfans et Less espaignols portent grand
nombre de vin des canaries et huille despaigne qui
est leur meilleur de traffic de marchandise A l'ocasion
dequoy Ilz commerce serons Jnotil pour eux Car less
yndiens estoient permis de planter vignes et olliviers
quves la forme que de sus estant less terres sy fertilles
et en toutes saisons Loy y donne aux vignes le fruict boy a manger

Lechozic qui est adire le Jeune homme sachemine a laboui^ou^l qui est la maisoy du pere
on est la gorioque qui est la fille quil aime prenant tous ses ynstrumens assauoir
soy canau ou bateau arc flechez hichorne ou filez a pecher poisson faisant lattraicte
auoir a fait laisse tous ses ynstrumens au pere e a la fille disant hai hai qui signifie comme bona porte ty bona Rappar
dedans une samarque ou lit e se repoz Jusquar au lendemain matin e le Jour
est bon viuprenant soy arc e ses flechez pour aller a la chasse au bois e aians donne se
proie lapporte en la maisoy la baillant a sa bien aimee ou amoureuse ps la conmodet
esfaire cuire ne beuuant ne mengeant en la maisoy e prennen se naien appor
de uiandes e benaisoy en abondance e en apporte le plus quil puist ps Monstrer il
est homme de grand deuoeur pour bien nourrir soy sa femme e famille

Come lyndien bien du bois apportant sa proie en la maison de
sa bien aimee

ᴣ le lendemain,
ᴣyndien venant du bois apporte sa proie en lagmaison —
Demourant et mangeant en Icelle avec le pere et la mere —
De son amoureuze en te souiana de lalliana qui se fraich —
Du mariage il luy et lacf fille.

Come Indien Sen va a la posche il

Lyndien prend son filets pour aller pescher
du poisson et l'aiant pesche l'apporte en la
maison de son amoureuse pour luy complaire y en
aiant grand nombre c'est bien peu de commun
a se resiouir du grand nombre de poisson par
luy apporté en la maison —

Come Les yndiens ſouluans a faire du Reſh
pour peſcher du poiſſon

L'indien a telle propriete en luy, quil fait derue-
ux manis du Reſh a peſcher du poiſſon et du-
samacquet qui ſont du liſt pour coucher et
ſont ſi experts que l'on ne Leur ſauroit monſtrer
œuure qu'ilz ne facent

Come Les Messagers yndiens dom portet lettres
par lé paÿs

Les yndiens messagers portens lettres fort longs dans le
paÿs ou les espaignols ne peuuent aller par terre les quels
boiageans on leur baille a portet Comme perdrix et
autre gibier pour faire presens aux gouuerneurs ausquelz
on enuoient parquels dtes lettres des flottes des nauires
qui arriuent aux yndes pour leur donne aduis et som
uieilles lettres portet au bou duy bastÿ fendu par le bou
quilz tiennent en leur main et par ce moien passent les
riuieres a nage sans mouiller lesy lettres et aut d'om

vne verge a laquelle jlz mettent leurs lettres ——
dedans cachetans lad verge auec dela cire pour ——
esuitter que leaue ny entre / Laquelle riuiere passee ——
ostent les lettres delad verge & les remettent ——
au bout dug baston Au moyen dequoy quand jlz treuuent
quelque yndiens par le chemin jlz nosent aprocher ——
du messagier portant les lettres & par ce qui leur
donne a entendre que cest vng esprit qui por —
Et estans les messagier arriue au lieu ou jl est ——
enuoie presente les lettres auec le gibier ou aultre ——
chose aluy baillee & sil est trouue quil y ait faulte de
perdrix & quil naie presente le contenu de ses lettres
Le seigneur ou gouuerneur a qui la chose est enuoiee ——
Demande aus messagier le deffault & a quil na tenu ——
Alors lindien luy demande qui luy a dit les deffaultz .
Lequel luy fait responce que cest vng esprit & par ——
lettres qui luy a reuellé Laquelle chose jl croist fermem[ent]

# HINDE·FESANTDVFEV·

Aux Indes se trouue vng Cotang bois fort beau
De Coulleur Jaulne Jl font vng pertuis au
Mitten et prenant vng bafton auec du cottoy
Le mettent dedans le pertuis et a force de
frotter entre leurs mains le baston le cotton
Contre led bois Le feu sengendre au Cottoy

Comme Les yndienā fillemēt coton

Les yndiens prengnent du coton en leur main auec
ung fuzeau et le uirdent sur leure cuisses auec
grand dilligenca et promphtitude a faire oeure de
Leure mains en en filleront pour Tour desme leure
Et en fons dela Thoulle dequoy Ilz se uestem

## CANA DEÇOI LES HINDES VONT ALAPAICHERIE

Et Comme Jlz peschent le poisson

Vont A la mer auec leur canau et ligne amaram
leur ligne a ung des costez du Canau Cela estant faict
prennent leurs lignes et les mettent sur leurs aureilles
et laultre a leur bouche puis sentam que le poisson et
prins promptimem auec leurs mains tirent leur ligne
et le poisson

La Maniere & faſon de Iardiner & planter
des yndiens

L'indien faiſant ſon Iardin ſemens pluſrs ſortes
de graynes pour ſa nourriture pour faire paroiſtre
qu'il eſt homme de grand trauail & auſſy pr complaire
a ſon amoureuſe & ſuffiſant pour nourrir femme & enffans
& la terre eſt ſy fructueuſe qu'elle porte du fruict en dix tmps

Come L'indien vient du bois apportans Mamie
Mamie est une Rachine deguoy l'on fait
du pain qui se nomme Cassaue happorte
aus a qui Couue dans le bois boy a Menger
Comme du oulcuurie noixes z audis chojer
pot sa nourriture

Come l'indien vanau bois cherchir des fruits

L'indien venant au bois apporte toutes sortes de
fruits quil trouve a menger pour la nourriture de
luy sa femme & famille & en apporte le plus
qui luy est possible

Come l'indien aiant fait fin de son trauail p̃ satisfaire & contenter
sa bien aimée se Joignent ensemble en Mariage apprez la demonstrãc̃
faicte par le pere de la fille comme orres & apprez ―

L'indien aiant fait le plus grand trauail qui luy est possible pour ̃ venir ―
Contentant a sa bien aimée S'acoustre le plus magnifiquement quil puist seullem̃ en
La maison du pere de la fille Lequel luy remonstre le grand trauail qui est
en luy & la bonne volonté quil a d'estre bien nourrie Quoy boiant, le pere remonstre
a sa fille en sa presence Luy disant Il te fault auoir ce Jeune homme Il te
nourrira bien Tu bibra quil apporte & grand nombre de biens pour nous nourrir
Il trauaille bien tant a pescher poisson prendre bestes sauuages fait Jardiner
va chercher fruits bois Bref tout ce quil fault pour la nourriture de la
maison Lequel pere aiant fait lad̃ remonstrance bien, pareillement remonstre
au Jeune homme comment sa fille trauaille bien tant a faire du pain acoustrer
la viande pour manger quelle fait cuire de dans Louille au tems dit
Lequel apprez auoir fait du feu sur remonstrances Ils se Joignent ensemble
au nom de mariage en la maison du pere & estans marier Le pere de la
mariée ne veullent plus riens faire pour eux mais & leurs enffans Les nourrissent
Il ny a aucune race en chacque billage Ils ne permettent qu'au tour de leur race
y demeurent Auquel billage Ils choisissent le plus ancien quil appelle

Cassicque qui est un tamz comme Roy auquel Ilz obeissent —
en toute chose Et lors quil adviendra Que leurs terres ne —
fructifient ou sont lassees de porter Ilz quictent Tout de
ses bons a autre lieu habiter ou Ilz labourent autre terre
ou Ilz scavent quil y a de leaue douce puis au bout de trois —
ou quatre ans retournent a leurs premieres terres ou Ilz —
sacommodent comme Ilz faisoient au paravant —

# TRANSLATIONS

## ACHE DES YNDES (GARLIC OF THE INDIES)

This is a garlic which is sweeter than that of France. It stays together and does not separate at all on touch like that of France. The Indians are very fond of it; they roast it on the fire like a pear and eat it.

## f. 3 (1 of 2)
### ANONNE (SOUR-SOP)

This fruit is found in the woods.

## f. 3 (2 of 2)
### ICAQVES (ICACO PLUM)

A fruit similar to plums and cherries growing in the garden of the Indians; it has stones having the taste of tender beans.

## f. 3v
### HAVOQATES (AVOCADO)

This fruit is found in the woods.

## f. 4 (1 of 2)
### HONNES (BERRIES)

Very large berries growing in the woods which taste like a bunch of grapes of which the Indians make use and eat them. They get drunk with them and lose their senses. This fruit grows without labor or sowing by man but naturally.

## f. 4 (2 of 2)
### PINNES (PINEAPPLE)

An exquisite fruit, extremely good, having the taste of raspberry; it grows on a tall tree where there can be found several, having the characteristic of growing rather down than up in contrast to the fruits of France. It is eaten raw with salt only to relieve the Indians of stomach pains.

## f. 4v
### PETVN (TOBACCO)

A special herb which the Indians use for food as well as an extremely beneficial medicine; when they are sick, they breathe in the smoke by mouth with a straw; soon the ill humour escapes by vomiting. They often pulverize it and, putting it in their noses, it distills several drops of water from the brain to discharge it. It also is found very helpful for toothache; laying its leaves on the teeth, the pain disappears; it is also beneficial for alleviating eye problems and, for this [purpose], it is advisable to take the herb and steep it in water about half of a quarter of an hour and then wash one's eyes and one will experience its benefit.

## AGOVQVES (CASSAVA)

This is a root which the Indians use to make bread; they call it cassava, which, when eaten before the sun sends its rays upon it, puts them in mortal danger; one can compare the root to a poison which the sun with its power purifies, and thus removes the danger.

## PRENNELLES (PRUNELLE, SLOE)

This is a fruit which is found in the wood and is very rare, having the particular virtue of quenching the thirst of the Indians. They are similar to the plums of France, having an orange color.

## AGOVIAMME (SQUASH)

It is grown from seeds which the Indians sow in their gardens. They live on this fruit letting it roast on their wood fires; it is excellent food for the Indians and there is plenty of it.

## PETONNES (BOTTLE-GOURD)

It is a fruit which grows in the gardens of the Indians in a region called Caribara; it is a very good and excellent fruit when it is ripe; they cook it over wood-embers and it provides them with good nourishment.

## INHAMES

Excellent good fruit.

## PINEVLLES

Fruit having the taste of cherries which the Indians use against thirst.

## TOMATES (TOMATO)

Very exquisite fruit growing in the wood and being cooked with fish and meat.

## SIROVELES

Extremely good fruit having the taste of dates and growing in the wood.

## MAMEE (MAMEE APPLE)

Fruit of outstanding goodness growing in the wood.

## GOVNAVE (SOURSOP)

This fruit is found in the woods.

## PRANNONQVES (AGAVE)

This is a fruit which grows in the woods, excellent and of great substance. The Indians take off the leaves around it, peeling it down to the white of the fruit, then let it roast on wood-embers and eat it, having the taste of an artichoke.

## GOVIAVES (GUAVA)

A fruit extremely useful for the bloody flux [dysentery]. Eaten still green, it relieves the person and, when ripe and smooth, it is a most excellent fruit.

## MAMONNE (SOUR-SOP, CUSTARD APPLE FAMILY)

Fruit growing in the woods and very excellent to eat, produced by a tree having a great many sharp points. The Indians therefore do not pick it; they rather beat it with a long stick having a cutting edge at its end.

## PATATES (SWEET POTATO)

The Indians use this fruit as excellent nourishment and cook it with meat in a pot or braise it; it originates in the earth; is shaped like a root, and one can multiply it by cutting small pieces which one plants like a seed which grows.

## PIMENTE (PIMENTO)

It is called in the language of the Indians "Hagis" and "poivre de Bresil" in French.

## COQVES (COCONUT TREE)

Fruit growing on a tree like a nut. After removal of the first shell two eyes and a mouth like those of a fish appear containing very good nourishment white in color. There also is within the shell an exquisite liquid for quenching the thirst of persons having a fever.

## f. 11v
### PLANTAINNES (PLANTAIN)

Good fruit similar to the grape vine. When a branch breaks off, it sprouts another; it has the shape of a long cucumber and has an extremely good taste, yet it causes flatulence. It is eaten cooked or raw and it is available at all times.

## f. 12 (1 of 2)
### PATILLE (WATERMELON)

It is a melon which is excellent for those who are unable to urinate; after eating it, the person will promptly and easily pass water. The Indians grow it from seed in their gardens.

## f. 12 (2 of 2)
### PAPAE (PAWPAW TREE)

Good fruit having the taste of a sugary melon and carrying seed similar to the hemp seed.

## f. 12v
### VENRAGIERE (EGGPLANT)

This fruit grows from seed. It is very good for chasing a person's bad blood being cooked with meat.

## f. 13
### CIBOLLES DES YNDES (ONIONS OF THE INDIES)

These are onions, sweet and very large, more so than those of France, being white inside and red outside. The Indians eat them as we eat apples—they have some all the time. They grow them from seed in their gardens and harvest them three times a year.

## f. 13 v
### MIL (MAIZE)

This is a grain which the Indians use for baking bread; after being ground in a wooden mortar, it yields a very white and very good flour; it is harvested three times a year.

## f. 14 (1 of 2)
### ACAGOVA (CASHEW NUT)

This fruit contains oil in its exterior. It is white inside and is a particularly hot meat.

## f. 14 (2 of 2)
### PALMITES (PALM-MARROW)

This is a very tall tree. When its bark is removed, it tastes similarly to cabbage cooked with good meat.

## f. 15
### BALCE

It is a resin very good for healing wounds inflicted by arrows and other ailments, being applied with tobacco. It also is very helpful in curing the bloody flux [dysentery] being taken with an egg.

## f. 15v
### FIGVE SAVVAGE (WILD FIG)

The Indians commonly eat this fruit; it grows in the woods.

## f. 16
### TORCHALES (CACTUS)

This is a tree which does not bear fruit nor leaves. It has a great many needles and is very hard and beautiful inside. It is veined verging on a shade of violet and has a very good and excellent fragrance.

## f. 17
### CABOVCLE (CABUYA)

This tree grows in the woods; the Indians make ropes and nets for fishing from it.

## f. 17v
### BREGELE

This herb serves to soften hard iron. They take the leaf and some soil which they call "a bar" and wrap the iron with said leaf. They cover it with earth and then throw it in the fire and the fire being sufficiently hot, it [the iron] becomes as soft as lead.

## f. 18 (1 of 2)
### PATATES DE LA MARGUERITE (SWEET POTATO FROM THE ISLA DE MARGARITA, VENEZUELA)

This fruit is also eaten instead of bread after being roasted over wood-embers.

## f. 18 (2 of 2)
### ROVMERRE

An herb very good for bad air. The Indians throw

it in the fire in their houses and burn it and if there are some poisonous animals of any sort when they smell the smoke of this herb, they die instantly and by the same method all the poison disappears.

### f. 18v
### CANBRE

This tree is useful for the bloody flux [dysentery]. One takes the leaf and pounds it together with salt and water in a mortar. As soon as they drink it they are cured.

### f. 19
### FRIGOLLES (BEANS)

That is to say beans, having the same pods. The fruit which grows in said pods is round like peas. The Indians sustain themselves on it; it is very good food growing in the woods. They lay the beans on the fire and when the pod feels the heat, it opens and they eat them, having the taste of chestnuts.

### f. 20
### AVILANNES BLANCHES GOMITES (WHITE PHYSIC NUT)

They may as well be called white nuts; they are not at all as strong nor as harmful to the stomach as the black ones. They don't make one vomit at all.

### f. 21
### AVILANNES NOIRES GOMITES (PHYSIC NUT)

They may as well be called nuts. There grows on this tree a sort of small nuts and there are two kinds, black ones and white ones. When a person has eaten them, he will throw out everything in his body above and below. When the Indians feel they have eaten something bad or a poisonous animal has touched them, they take these nuts, promptly throwing out all the poison by mouth and "below" and are cured.

### f. 22
### HAGIS ROGES, HAGIS IANNE, HAGIS VERT (RED PEPPER, YELLOW PEPPER, GREEN PEPPER)

Hagis means pepper in the language of the Indians and there are three kinds. However, the smallest, which is green, is the strongest and its leaf is very good when added to soup and salad. The Indians mash this pepper with salt and put it in the husk of millet and when they go far away where they cannot find fresh water to drink, they eat as much as possible of this pepper en route and are not thirsty, feeling always fresh in spite of the very intense heat and their being nude.

### f. 23 (1 of 2)
### CHATANE DES INDES (CHESTNUT [?] OF THE INDIES)

This fruit grows along the water.

### f. 23 (2 of 2)
### MENNIL (CASSAVA)

This is a root which grows on the Isla de Margarita [Venezuela] where, once gathered, they dry it in the sun and then eat it like bread.

### f. 23v
### PATATES (SWEET POTATO)

The Indians make them into a beverage; after having boiled them in water, they squeeze them out with their hands and they get drunk as with wine.

### f. 24 (1 of 2)
### MIEL SAVVAGE (WILD HONEY TREE)

It is called wild honey tree, growing in the woods. They cook it with palm marrow and eat it like very excellent bread.

### f. 24 (2 of 2)
### BARBEQVE

This tree grows in Florida; it is orange inside and has an excellent odor like a rose. The Indians boil it and make paint from it with which they paint men and women to make them more beautiful.

### f. 24v
### PITE (SILK-GRASS)

This tree grows in the country of Le Rayne [Colombia] in the Magdalena River, also called the Great River. They extract from it material to make a beautiful thread like silk having the color of silver.

### f. 25
### MADAE (MADERA)

It is a tree which bears no fruit. It is the most beautiful wood one can see when it is stripped. It is among the hardest wood of all that can be found, having purple color inside and being veined and beautiful par excellence; it also has a good odor.

## f. 26
### CARANE
This is a very excellent resin for curing any pain of the chest being applied in the form of a plaster on the most painful spot.

## f. 27
### MENSENILLE (MANCHINEEL TREE)
A very poisonous tree, so that if a person looks up to it, he will be blinded for three hours afterwards. The Indians hide their arrows in this tree when they are at war in order to make them poisonous.

## f. 27v
### CANIFISTE
Very good fruit for the sick having been preserved when small; the Indians use it together with Pimento as remedy for their illnesses.

## f. 28 (1 of 2)
### LACIQVE
Herb very appropriate for relieving those hurt by work. Being boiled with water, it is rubbed on the sole of one's foot and the palm of one's hand to get rid of any pain.

## f. 28 (2 of 2)
### SACAFRAS (SASSAFRAS)
Tree growing in Florida very much in the interior. The Indians make wine from its root which is as good as cinnamon and equally excellent as Muscadet and it grows throughout the Cape St. Augustine.

## f. 28v
### CACINE (ILEX CASSINE, HOLLY TREE)
This tree grows in Florida very much in the interior. The Indians collect the leaves to make a very good beverage after having boiled them with water. They keep it for one year and get drunk as with wine.

## f. 29
### MIATÓNA
This is a tree which grows in the water—and bears a very excellent black seed for dying silk of

black color which is very beautiful. The Indians ordinarily dye their cotton clothes with it.

## f. 30
### CHUPPE
This is a tree which grows in the midst of the forest and bears a very excellent fruit. The Indians don't dare venture out to look for it on account of the tigers and snakes. The snakes suck the fruit in and eat it when it has fallen to the ground.

## f. 31
### COVCHEQVOV (COUSCOUS)
This is a sort of grain which is very good—it is similar to rice. The Indians sow it in their gardens just like wheat and nourish themselves on it, harvesting it twice a year.

## f. 32
### COMME LE COTON CROIST AUX ARBRES (HOW THE COTTON GROWS ON TREES)
Cotton grows on this tree in the woods. The Indians make with it hedges to close off their gardens and inside the cotton is a small black seed which produces cotton and which increases in size.

## f. 33
### PALME (PALM TREE)
Tree from which the Indians draw wine having the taste of perry; they cut the trees nearby giving shade so that the sun can give its warmth more intensively, for the stronger the sun the more wine has the tree. They also pierce said tree to its heart in order to make the wine gush out and even make a big fire to keep away the poisonous beasts.

## f. 34
### PIAHOVNA
This is a sort of mussel in which grows a fish—similar to a conger-eel which has the head of a snake. It is found in fresh water streams and is not good eating because it is bitter, reeking of mud—oily and sweetish.

## f. 35 (1 of 2)
### SADRE (SEA BREAM)
Sadre fish of the Indies.

*DORADE (FISH WITH GOLDEN SCALES)*

Dorade a beautiful fish and excellent eating.

*f. 42v*

*BONNITE (BONITO)*

Bonito, a very good tasting fish.

*f. 43 (1 of 2)*

*CONCHE (CONCH)*

This may as well be called a shell and it grows in a bay which is beside the sea which is called Baillahonde [on the Guajire Peninsula in Colombia] into which empty fresh water rivers. The fish which grows inside is very good and dainty; the shell is red in color on top and violet inside.

*f. 43 (2 of 2)*

*CONCHE (CONCH)*

This shell is beautiful; it is very rough on top. The Indians use it to grind ginger and peanuts, which is a root from which they make flour which serves them instead of bread.

*f. 44*

*CANAV DE LA MER DV SVS (CANOE OF THE SOUTH SEA)*

This canoe is from the South Sea from an island called Gilolo where Francis Drake, an English man, had his ship cleaned to make it ready for his voyage of the South Sea.

*f. 44v (1 of 2)*

*SETAQVE*

This is a green-colored stone which is found among the sea beds where they fish for pearls, that is at La Margarita. It gives off a sound like glass and is very excellent for all pain of the flanks, being laid on the painful side.

*f. 44v (2 of 2)*

*HOVITRE DE LORANBEC (OYSTER FROM LORANBEC)*

*f. 45*

*CANAV DANTIGOVA (CANOE OF ANTIGUA)*

The Indians use this fish to catch others. They first tame it by feeding it when it is small and when they want to fish, they feed this fish on the gland of a cayman then throw it in the sea having tied a string to its tail. When the fish smell the odor of the glands it has eaten, they come close to it and the Indians slowly pull the string to bring the fish near the boat; the fish is followed by others and, at this instant, they throw out the net and all the fish which followed the other fish are caught.

*f. 46*

*CHVCET (CHUCET FISH)*

This is a fish which is hard to cook and the longer one boils it, the harder it becomes; being out of the water it is used to, on land or on the deck of the ship, it clings with the underside of its throat to land or wood in such a way that it is not possible to pull it off without killing it.

*f. 47 (1 of 2)*

*MANTTE (MANTA RAY)*

This fish is very large and no less vicious. When the negroes dive in the sea for pearls it jumps on them to make them drown and afterwards eats them.

*f. 47 (2 of 2)*

*CONCHE (CONCH)*

It grows where one fishes for pearls. In this conch is found a certain hair like human hair the color of gold and it is very excellent for people who have an earache or who are somewhat deaf. They dry it in the sun and then put it in their ears and immediately feel its benefit. The negroes often use it, their ears being hurt by frequent dives.

*f. 48 (1 of 2)*

*HIOGANE (IGUANA)*

This is a very dangerous sea and land serpent whose bite is incurable.

*f. 48 (2 of 2)*

*CHATILLE (SEAL)*

This fish lives in the sea and in fresh water in the land of Lorembec [Loranbec] between Florida and Terre Neuve [Newfoundland] and is worthless as food.

*f. 48v*

*CHEVAL MARIN (SEA HORSE)*

This animal is found on the Isla de Margarita where one fishes for pearls.

### f. 49 (1 of 2)
### HOMMAR (LOBSTER)

It is found in the sea at an island called Bastimentos between Nombre de Dios and the River Sagre, being violet in color and having red claws.

### f. 49 (2 of 2)
### CAXQVENOC (HORSESHOE CRAB)

Crab of Florida.

### f. 49v
### CARACOLLE (SNAIL)

### f. 50
### CRATON PORC ESPIC DE MER (CRATON, PORCUPINE OF THE SEA)

This is a very dangerous fish. The other fish hide and flee from it and its whole body is covered with spines like the bristles of a porcupine.

### f. 51
### PATONNE (PATONNE FISH)

This is a fish very excellent for eating having the taste of sturgeon and often living in fresh water rivers.

### f. 52 (1 of 2)
### TORTVE NICOTE (TORTOISE)

This fish lives in the woods close to the sea.

### f. 52 (2 of 2)
### TORTVE (TURTLE)

Fresh water turtle found in Florida and very excellent eating.

### f. 52v
### VIVREE (WEEVERFISH)

This animal lives in the woods and in fresh water rivers and is very poisonous. The Indians use it to poison their arrows when they go to war.

### f. 53 (1 of 2)
### TORTVE (TURTLE)

This fish is four feet long and two and a half feet wide. According to the reports of sailors it can live up to a hundred and fifty years. It is found on Cayman Island and lives in the sea as well as on land. It lays a large number of eggs and is good to eat.

### f. 53 (2 of 2)
### CAIAMANT (CROCODILE)

Marine, this fish is terrestrial and aquatic. It is found between the mainland and Cayman Island where there is no human settlement only a great number of these fishes with large turtles.

### f. 53v
### CAIAMANT (RIVER CAIMAN)

This fish lives in the woods and fresh water rivers. It has in its head a peculiar stone for those persons suffering from gravel (in their urine) or from kidney stones. The Indians put the stone in the fire until it is all red, then, in order to cool it, they put it in the potion or drink of the person affected with gravel. The patient having drunk it, the stones which he ejects are broken up in his body and reduced to mud. It (the animal) also has four glands under its armpits giving an excellent perfume.

### f. 54 (1 of 3)
### COVLLEVVRE NOIRE (BLACK SNAKE)

Being nine or ten feet long they are good eating.

### f. 54 (2 of 3)
### RACELLE (RACELLE ROOT)

This root serves the Indians well when bitten by the snake. Even when they pursue them in the woods to bite and injure them, they throw some of this same root in front of the snakes which instantly withdraw.

### f. 54 (3 of 3)
### COVLLEVVRE BLANCHE (WHITE SNAKE)

Very poisonous and dangerous. Finding Indians in the woods they attack them in order to harm them.

### f. 55 (1 of 2)
### PIOVCHE DE MER

This is as valuable as a louse.

*ETOVELLE DE MER (STARFISH)*

This fish is worthless as food, being very poisonous. Its usual retreat is still water.

*PIRRAVGVE DE LA MARGVERITE,
PIRRAVGVE DE LA TRENITE (CANOE
OF MARGARITA ISLAND, CANOE OF
TRINIDAD)*

These canoes are fighting each other and when the
enemy has been caught, he is a prisoner all his life.
When waging war, they take their women with
them; they pull the oar while their husbands fight.

*CANAV POUR PECHER LES PERLES
(CANOE FOR PEARL-FISHING)*

Pearls are being fished in the ocean between the
main-land and Isla de Margarita, approximately
ten leagues, in three or four fathoms of water by
the negroes who dive into the sea, holding a hoop-
net to descend to the bottom where they scrape the
soil where the oysters are, in order to find the
pearls. And the deeper they descend in the water,
the larger are the pearls they find. Not being able
to hold their breath longer than a quarter of an
hour, they come up again and pull their hoop-net.
The fishing from morning to evening having been
completed, they return to La Rancheria where
they live. Pearls are being fished in three places,
namely, on Isla de Margarita, in Riohacha, and at
the Cabo de la Vela.

*HOVITRE HOV CROICE LES PERLES
(OYSTER IN WHICH PEARLS GROW)*

Oyster in which the pearls grow.

*CRAPAVLT BELANT (BLEATING
TOAD)*

Its blood is very poisonous with which, together
with its brain, the Indians poison their arrows
applying them with the leaf from the mensenille
tree [Manchineel Tree].

*CENT PIERNE (CENTIPEDE)*

A very poisonous beast. It feeds in places where

there is wine or vinegar. It only moves around at
night. A person who has been bitten by this animal lives only for twenty-four hours afterwards. It
finds the Indians in their beds in order to kill them.

*PA*

Animal which is highly prized as food by the
Indians. It is grey and white in color.

*PORC DE MONTENNE (MOUNTAIN
PIG)*

This animal is called a mountain pig because it
lives in the mountains. It is adroit in climbing. It
has a navel on its back.

*TIGRE FERMILLIERE (TIGER AND
ANTEATER)*

Savage beast. However, whenever this small animal called anteater encounters a tiger looking for
prey it turns on its back and throws itself on the
tiger's neck and pierces its throat with its snout
and claws and does not release him until he is dead
on that spot.

*CABRITE SAVVAGE (FERAL GOAT)*

Living in the woods, it is very excellent eating.

*CIFRE (MONKEY)*

This is a very agile beast. The Indians cannot
tame it or feed it for they die of grief and do not eat
in captivity. They have a face like a human and are
very mischievous and rebellious and throw themselves against people mainly at their faces and eyes.

*PATIA (DEER)*

This is an animal that lives in the woods. It has the
body of a goat, but a very long one. It grazes like
a goat, is excellent eating, it is easy to tame. The
Indians keep it in their houses.

*MONTONS DU PEROV (SHEEP OF
PERU)*

These sheep are used by the Spaniards instead of

horses to carry their gold and silver from the mines to the towns near the sea. There they are put on ships and taken to Spain when the fleet of the Indies sets out. They (the sheep) are big and strong. They jostle the people and make them fall down. They are very good at climbing the mountains of the country which the horses could not do, and when these sheep have arrived at the towns of their destination they are sold to the master of the ship or another merchant as provision.

## f. 63
### CHAPPOU (WILD CAT)

This is a wild cat which is found in the woods. It is an evil beast, agile and quick to climb trees. It hunts small animals like hares, rabbits and other small animals living in the woods which make up most of its diet.

## f. 64
### PERIQITE LEGERE (SLOTH)

The nature of this animal is to climb with its belly uppermost and, climbing this way, it moves faster than a man could on foot. The skin of this animal is very excellent for people suffering from the falling sickness [epilepsy]. The head of the afflicted is covered with it and then one realizes how effective the skin is.

## f. 65 (1 of 2)
### SAGOVAI (MONKEY)

This animal is found in the country called La Rayne [Colombia].

## f. 65 (2 of 2)
### CRABLE SAVVAGE (SCORPION)

It is a very poisonous animal which lives close to horses and mules. It has a stinger at the end of its mouth and when it has stung a horse or mule, they die immediately.

## f. 66
### PERRE SIMARRON (WILD DOG)

One may as well call them wild dogs which are found in the woods and hunt small pigs and calves and eat them, living only on animals. They normally are in the woods to find food. Bulls, cows and pigs produce their little ones in the woods. These dogs are difficult to tame being fierce and

mean and one can only tame them if one catches them young or kills them.

## f. 67
### VACHE BRAVE (FERAL COW)

This is a very wild and raging cow and when it is excited none of the Indians dares come near it and they cannot tame it. Normally it lives in woods with the wild beasts. It is sired by a bull and a female deer since bulls normally are in the woods where they find their pasture.

## f. 68 (1 of 2)
### CHOVLECQVE

This is an animal that wages war on hares and rabbits like the fox in this country [France]. It has two glands like a civet cat producing a very excellent perfume which is similar to that of a sheep's droppings and the skin has a very good scent.

## f. 68 (2 of 2)
### CHVPA (ARMADILLO)

This is an animal that lives underground like a badger. It only feeds on roots and no animal dares attack it since it retracts head and paws in a ball in its shell similar to that of a tortoise. Its meat is very excellent eating.

## f. 69 (1 of 2)
### MONNE BARBVE (BEARDED MONA)

This animal is the size of a greyhound. When it sees people in the woods it breaks off branches and throws them at the men. Their habitat is normally in the forests between Nombre de Dios and Panama.

## f. 69 (2 of 2)
### PORC EPIC SAVVAGE (WILD PORCUPINE)

## f. 70 (1 of 2)
### AGATILLE SAVVAGE (WILD AGATILLE)

This animal is found in Florida and produces much musk perfume. It also has a beautiful pelt with spots of brown, red, and grey color.

## f. 70 (2 of 2)
### FLEQVE

This animal is very nimble in climbing trees and

eating in the water so that it wages war against the fish in the rivers.

### f. 71 (1 of 2)
#### TATOVAI (ARMADILLO)

This animal burrows into the ground like rabbits. It lives on roots and is very good food.

### f. 71 (2 of 2)
#### AGOVTIA (AGOUTI)

Dangerous animal living in the woods.

### f. 72
#### MOVQVITES (MOSQUITO)

They are small flies which are so small that one cannot see them, they are very dangerous. When there is no wind and the weather is calm, they come in droves attacking people, stinging them in such a manner that one would take them for lepers. Where they bite, the flesh swells up like a pea and if one kills said flies where they have stung, this protects them from the swelling. The Indians make a fire in their houses in order to keep them away and they only appear at night, retreating during the day close to the sea in the sand.

### f. 73
#### AIGLE PIERRE (EAGLE STONE)

Of the Indies; this bird carries in his stomach a very peculiar stone for women in child-bed. In order to use the stone, it is proper to lay it on the left thigh of the woman and she will promptly give birth.

### f. 74 (1 of 2)
#### MARGANAHV

Bird living in the woods is very excellent food.

### f. 74 (2 of 2)
#### POVLLE DV PEROV (HEN FROM PERU)

This bird takes shelter in smoky places where one makes a fire and when it can get into a garden it eats the melons.

### f. 75 (1 of 2)
#### FLAMANT (FLAMINGO)

Bird good to eat.

### f. 75 (2 of 2)
#### FAVLTQVET (SHEARWATER)

This bird is very oily. It burrows in the ground like a rabbit.

### f. 76 (1 of 2)
#### CEQQVAHONASO (TOUCAN)

This bird's beak is bigger than the rest of its body.

### f. 76 (2 of 2)
#### PERDRIS DES INDES (PARTRIDGE OF THE INDIES)

They are violet-colored and very excellent eating.

### f. 77 (1 of 2)
#### GRANT GOSIER (PELICAN)

Its gullet is bigger than the rest of its body holding nearly a pail of water or other liquid. It lives in the rivers and feeds on fish. Its size is that of a gosling.

### f. 77 (2 of 2)
#### NOGALINAGE

This bird is similar to a crow. It lives on carrion and usually dies of heat and thirst.

### f. 78 (1 of 2)
#### MOVCHE (FIREFLY)

Of the Indies; it has such power as to give a light at night so strong that one can easily recognize people from a distance of two or three paces, and it flies in the air.

### f. 78 (2 of 2)
#### CATALI

Bird from the South Sea.

### f. 79 (1 of 2)
#### GAGEAV

This is a wild bird that wages war against the other birds. It is very wild, it lives in the woods, and when the Indians have caught some young ones they can never tame them. Being angry they throw themselves at people.

### f. 79 (2 of 2)
#### PATE

This is a bird that lives in fresh water and is very good food. The Indians catch them at night by means of a fire, and seeing said fire, they come close. The Indians set out bait, and with nets made from strings, they catch a great number of them.

### f. 81
### CASIQVE (CACIQUE)

This type of man is called Cacique. He is very much like a king to whom is paid honor and obedience and, to be recognized, they wear a ring hanging from their nose and a band on the forehead as you see it here on the picture, band and ring of gold, not tolerating—he as well as his subjects, as is their custom—any hair on their face or on their private parts, keeping only the hair on their head which they grow long to protect themselves from the heat of the sun.

### f. 82
### HINDIANE (WOMAN OF THE INDIES)

This woman chases the flies with a little bell hanging from a tree branch, afraid that when they bite their children, they will cry, for seeing their children cry makes them very sad, having visions that at that time the devil is in their body. The flies, although small, astonishingly sting the Indians which causes a large swelling like a pea, but being killed immediately and on the bite, they are cured.

### f. 83
### HINDE DE LA TRENITE (INDIAN OF TRINIDAD)

The manner of catching parrots is this: if they are large, they make a trap with a string attached to it. In this trap they put a parrot with his feet tied and next to him a small animal called catille which plucks him. When the parrot cries and the other parrots, hearing his voice, come to his rescue, freely joining him in the trap, the Indian seeing this pulls the string and the parrots are instantly trapped.

### f. 84
### HINDIANE (WOMAN OF THE INDIES)

This woman catches fish in the ocean to feed her husband and children.

### f. 85
### HINDES DE IHONA (INDIANS OF IHONA)

When the Indians have defeated their enemies, they make them lie down on the ground, then pound on them and, after that, give them a blow on the head with their sword. When the blood starts flowing, they hold it back promptly, thinking that by this means the body will make a better roast for a solemn feast, calling this a deed of prowess.

### f. 86
### HINDIANE (WOMAN OF THE INDIES)

This woman beats the wheat kernel in a wooden mortar and produces a very white flour from which they make very good and very nourishing bread.

### f. 87
### HINDEDE S MATRE (INDIAN OF SANTA MARTA)

These Indians are handsome and strong men, artful in war, among the other Indians from the region of Bahia Honda (on the peninsula of La Guajira, Colombia). They assemble for combat up to eighty thousand men and when their enemies are wounded by their arrows, they only survive twenty-four hours because the arrows are strongly poisoned.

### f. 88
### HINDE DE NIQVEAVGVE (INDIAN OF NICARAGUA)

This is one way of catching parrots. They use an arrow with a cotton pad at the end and when the bird is struck, it does not die, but only falls, being dazed.

### f. 89
### HINDE DE CARIBARA (INDIAN OF CARIBARA)

To test whether their poison is effective, they aim their arrows at a tree and then retract them. When the poison is effective, the tree drops its leaves and dies in less than half a day. To make their poison, they mix the leaf of a tree called mensenille, the blood of a bleating toad, and the flesh of a centipede, mashing the whole, put it in a small clay pot, cover it carefully and bury it in the ground for six "limes," which is about six months. When the time is passed, they test the arrows as you see here.

### f. 90
### HINDE DE LORANBEC (INDIAN OF LORANBEC)

These Indians dressed in skins are extremely skillful in battle on account of their strength, as the

English could tell fighting under Sir Francis Drake in 1586 when they attempted to conquer this land, but were forced to weigh anchor and retreat because of the resistance they encountered. Its location is between Florida and Terre Neuve [Newfoundland] at 36½ latitude.

### f. 91
### COM̃E LE BLED CROIST EN VNE PROUINCE NOMMEE LERESNE PAIS-DES YNDES DU PEROU . . . (HOW THE WHEAT GROWS IN A PROVINCE CALLED LERESNE, LAND OF THE INDIANS OF PERU, BEING TWO HUNDRED LEAGUES INSIDE THE COUNTRY WHERE A RIVER CALLED LA MAGDALENA, ALSO CALLED THE GREAT RIVER, ORIGINATES, WHICH IS SEVEN LEAGUES WIDE AND EMPTIES FRESH WATER INTO THE SEA FOR A GOOD LEAGUE AND A HALF)

This province is fertile in wheat, meat, fowl, gold, and gems, like emeralds and other precious stones, and, with these, is found plenty of rock crystal. The Indians ordinarily harvest wheat twice a year which they take to other places where there is none at all, completely ground by them, and put it into sacks filled to capacity, sending them by sea and land in exchange for wine from the Canaries, linen, knives, hoops, and other things which they need, like fish-hooks, because they have only those made of fish-bone.

### f. 92
### HINDE FLECHER (INDIAN WOUNDED BY ARROW)

When the Indians are mortally wounded by arrows, one lays them on a rack and makes an oven with a tube leading to the wound of the sick man. When the fire is lighted, they put in it a leaf of tobacco together with a resin called bal-sam and as soon as the smoke enters the wound of the patient, they take a leaf of tobacco with some of the balsam and make a plaster which they apply to the wound of the patient, and he is cured.

### f. 93–93v
### LISLE APPELLEE FOUGUE OU JSLE DE

### FEU (ISLAND CALLED "FOUGUE" OR FIRE ISLAND)

This island, according to the estimation of the navigators, is three or four leagues high. During the day one always sees smoke on top and when the sun has set and night has come, one likewise sees a great fiery blaze because on the island and on the summit, the earth produces sulfur and there is thunder and lightning which cause the continu-ous fire. This island is located in the ocean and is one of the Cape Verde Islands, a place 10 leagues or so from the mainland. In the lower part and along the island a great number of pumice stones are found floating in the sea which is frequented by few people. Since the place is deserted and almost infertile, it is besides dangerous for the nav-igators who are afraid to approach closer than two leagues on account of the sea being very high.

### f. 93v–94
### LISLE DES CAYAMANS (CAYMAN ISLAND)

This island is located in the ocean and is one of the islands of the mainland of Peru on which nobody lives because there is no fresh water and also because the soil does not produce any goods except a great number of caymans and turtles which live in the sea as well as on land. When these [the caymans] are ready to have little ones, they throw out their eggs through their mouth because nature did not provide an opening in their behind and this occurs on the sand close to the sea. They have the habit of covering the eggs with sand with their paws in order to protect them and when the sun warms them, little caymans are formed which are ravenous and dangerous in the sea as well as on land so that people are afraid to swim in the sea because of them. For when they hold a man, he cannot escape being carried off and eaten. The meat of the cayman is not valued as food, being dull and flavorless. On the other hand, the meat of the turtle is good eating. It has the habit when it wants to have little ones of throwing out the eggs in great abundance through its behind on the sand. They are yellow like the yolk of a hen's egg, round like a tennis-ball and without a shell, having only a white jelly all around it. They cover the eggs with sand like the cayman and when the sun shines on them, little turtles are formed which are excellent food. Even the eggs they produce have as much taste as those of a hen and are, besides, big and capacious, having a hard and thick shell. If one wants to take these, it is advisable to turn the turtle on its back. Being unable to move, one can take a great number. All around the island grow and are produced a great number of sponges good for washing oneself.

### f. 95v–f. 96
### LA MANIERE COMME LES YNDES VONT A LA CHASSE POUR PRENDRE LES LAPPINS (THE WAY THE INDIANS CHASE AND CATCH RABBITS)

They make an enclosure with a fence like a hurdle which they call in their language barbacone, cutting the grass where the rabbits come to rest, and looking from which side the wind blows, they make a fire there. The rabbits smelling it run and when they come to the end of said fence, the Indians are waiting for them there and kill them with their sticks.

### f. 96v
### COMME LES YNDES FONT LA CHASSE AU POISSON (HOW THE INDIANS HUNT FOR FISH)

The Indians go to the seashore and seeing a fish playing outside the water, quickly shoot at it with their arrows, making it die for when it is struck, it can no longer swim nor go to the bottom of the water.

### f. 97–97v
### LE PORT APPELLE' LE NOMBRE DE DIEU (PORT CALLED NOMBRE DE DIOS)

This is a beautiful and spacious harbor having a depth of seven to eight fathoms of water in which the fleet of ships from Spain arrives to trade merchandise with those from Peru which is located in a mountainous region where the air is heavy and unhealthy and the Spaniard cannot live there for a long time. For this reason, because they are not used and accustomed to the air of the country, it is advisable that these Spaniards abstain from wine without water and from eating oranges on account of the high fevers which are common there. In this port arrive gold and silver from Peru to be traded for merchandise with the Spaniards, gold and Reales being given in exchange for merchandise. They are afraid to have the gold and silver transported by land from Panama which is located in the Southern Sea and eighteen leagues from Nombre de Dios because of the runaway negro slaves who steal and plunder everything they find on the road belonging to the Spaniards. These runaway negroes form bands for fear to be surprised by the Spaniards. It is necessary that the traders coming from Panama to Nombre de Dios pass three fresh water rivers, the water covering half their bodies and they are in danger when the water is high. Men and mules carrying merchandise as well as gold and silver coins are usually submerged in the water.

### f. 98–98v
### COME LES ESMERAUDES CROISSENT ET SE RECOUURENT AUX MONTAIGNES (HOW EMERALDS GROW AND ARE MINED IN THE MOUNTAINS)

The precious stone called emerald grows on the very high mountains and the negro slaves have great trouble and difficulty obtaining it by reason of the height of the mountains. They usually end their days there because while digging in the rocks masses of stone fall on them which pin them underneath and they die miserably. There also is found a great quantity of beautiful rock crystal in large pieces richly adulterated with gold. These mountains are located in a province called Lerayne [Colombia] close to a city called Santa Fe, the capital of the province. This is a region rich in wheat, meat, fowl, and plenty of gold. The Indians of this region are good workers with great skill and intelligence, working and making beautiful cloth of fine wool with which the Spaniards dress and fit themselves out, having it dyed in various colors.

### f. 99–99v
### COME LES YNDIENS CHERCHENT LOR PROCEDANT DES MONTAIGNES LORS QUIL Y A JNONDATION DE'AUES VENANS DU CIEL (HOW THE INDIANS TRY TO FIND GOLD COMING FROM THE MOUNTAINS

WHEN THERE ARE FLOODS FROM
THE SKY)

The mountains of this region are very high, esti-
mated by the navigators to be close to four or five
leagues high up to their peaks, so that the slaves,
negroes as well as Indians, are unable to climb
them on account of their steepness and cold temperature. In these mountains there is up high a
great quantity of gold which is recovered and
found in the falling rain which forms small brooks
carrying much gold in small grains from the
heights which the Indians collect at the foot of the
mountains in small bowls as you see here above. It
represents great wealth and convenience beyond
the fact that the water coming down from the
mountains is extremely good for drinking and
does not harm a person. It is even very nourishing
for having passed through gold and has besides a
particular virtue so that whoever drinks it urinates
promptly and frees his kidneys of gravel and other
things.

### f. 100–100v
### COME LES ESCLAUES NAIGRES
### TRAUAILLENT ET CHERCHENT LOR
### AUX-MYNES EN LA TERRE NOMMEE
### VERAUGUE (HOW THE NEGRO
### SLAVES WORK AND LOOK FOR
### GOLD IN THE MINES OF THE REGION
### CALLED VERAGUA [PANAMA])

This region is very dangerous. The negroes live
there only a short time and no day and night pass-
es without rain, lightning and thunder because
this land is so close to the equinoctial line. Being
not fertile in goods, it has however a great deal of
good gold. The King of Spain permits the
Spaniards in the Indies to settle to build mines and
own the gold in them as long as they pay him the
tribute of a fifth of everything they find, of gold,
silver, as well as of precious stones. The Spaniards
do not force nor permit the Indians to work in the
mines for fear they should know the value of the
gold for, knowing it, they would go to war and
chase them out of the country. The Spaniards buy
a great number of negroes from Africa to serve
them as slaves and when the negroes have finished
a day's work in a group of eight or ten, there is at
the exit of these mines half a barrel filled with
water in which they wash the gold. Then they put
it in an iron bowl and place it on the fire to dry it.

When it is dry, they take it to the Major-domo,
whom they call "Maître d'hôtel," in order to see
and know from the weight how much it is. They
have to give him, as tribute, the value of the gold
amounting to the weight of three ducats for each
day. If it happens that they do not find in one day
the weight in gold of three ducats, they are liable
nevertheless to pay the tribute to the Major-domo.
If it happens also that they recover a larger
amount, it will be their gain.

### f. 101
### COME LES YNDIENS CHERCHENT
### LOR EN LA TERRE FERME DES
### YNDES NOMMÉE BORBORAT (HOW
### THE INDIANS LOOK FOR GOLD ON
### THE MAINLAND OF THE INDIES
### CALLED BORBORAT)

There is in this region also a great deal of gold.
The Indians do not allow the Spaniards who are
experts in war to settle there, the gold being of low
value. When the Indians trade with the
Spaniards, they give three ounces of gold for one
as they [the three ounces] are only worth one
ounce of gold at the price of twenty-two carats.
Besides, the Indians, ingenious as they are, make
and fashion in gold relief several kinds of animals
for their enjoyment which is something unbelievable to us since they are taught only by nature
which induces them to do this.

### f. 102–102v
### LA FORGE ROIALLE ET ORDINAIRE
### OU SE FONT LOR PROUENANT DES
### MYNES | EERIGEE PAR LE ROY
### DESPAIGNE | A FIN DELEUER SES
### TRIBUTZ (THE ROYAL OR ORDINARY
### FORGE WHERE THE GOLD COMING
### FROM THE MINES IS MADE. ERECTED
### BY THE KING OF SPAIN TO LEVY HIS
### TRIBUTE.)

It is not permitted nor legal for anyone, whoever it
is, negro, Spaniard, or Indian, to have a forge or
furnace to smelt the gold coming out of the mines.
They are obliged to bring it to the Royal Forge to
pay the tribute to the King of Spain which
amounts to a fifth of everything. Having paid the
tribute to the Major-domo, called Maître d'hôtel,
who receives the tribute, he stamps the gold of the
coins with the arms of the King of Spain in order

to show that the tribute has been paid and adds above the value of the gold after it has been assayed, namely whether it is worth twenty, twenty-one, or twenty-two carats so the people know its price. When it is found that there is no royal stamp by the King of Spain and the tribute has not been paid, the gold is confiscated and everything else, such as silver, precious stones and pearls; before passing from the Indies to Spain, they must register at the *contrestation* the amount of gold, silver, gems and pearls they take out of the country.

### f. 103–103v
### LE FOURNEAU ORDONNE POUR LA FONTE DELARGENT VENANT DES MYNES (THE FURNACE PRESCRIBED FOR THE SMELTING OF THE SILVER COMING FROM THE MINES)

This furnace is placed high and is being heated with a great deal of wood and charcoal which is put inside. The Indians take two bellows and blow into them with great force to make the furnace hot. They put the silver inside which is being melted and, in order to soften it, they throw a stone called tuf (or tufa), yellow in color, into the furnace which is very bright and has the capacity of softening the silver. They also put dead dogs and other carrion into the furnace and with the strong stench of the carrion and the help of the stone, they remove the bad quality of the silver, making it soft. When it has been melted, one of the Indians pierces the furnace with an iron rod through an opening at ground-level at the bottom of the foresaid furnace. The silver flows into the proper clay molds forming silver plaques and bars. Also when the silver is so refined that it is even softer, they make Reales, the coins of Peru, from it which show the impression of a small cross and the royal arms of Spain. They usually trade with them, and if they do not have silver coins, they give the weight in silver of three Reales for two coins, all this being good revenue and value for the King of Spain.

### f. 104
### COM͂E LES YNDIENS TRAUAILLENT AUX MINES DARGENT EN LA TERRE DU PEROU (HOW THE INDIANS

### *WORK IN THE SILVER MINES OF PERU)*

Silver grows deep in the soil like iron ore in France. The Indians find great quantities working in the mines in a group of eight to ten persons every day. The mines are far in the interior of the country, close to a city called Lima, capital of Peru. This silver is very sour coming from the mine and not fine, having the quality of tin and copper. But silver from the mines of New Spain is fine as it originates in better soil than that of Peru. The wives of the Indians carry the silver from the mines to the furnace for smelting and refining.

### f. 106–106v
### LA RIUIERE DE CHAGEE (THE CHAGRES RIVER)

This river has been recently discovered by the Spaniards. It serves their shipping and carries gold and silver from the port of Panama distant by three leagues over land from Cap La Cruz in Panama and is the beginning of said river. When the fleet of ships from Peru arrives in Panama laden with gold and minted silver, they carry the gold and silver on mules over land to the Port of La Cruz in order to ship it in barges on said river to Nombre de Dios, thus avoiding the danger from the runaway negro slaves, commonly called thieves, from the port of La Cruz to the entrance of the sea which is the end of the river, a distance of approximately nine leagues. The barges do not take long at all to come down to the sea and to be on the way to Nombre de Dios on account of the river's strong current. The barges are all laden with gold and silver and have only eight to ten negro slaves who swim when there is no proper wind, and one Spaniard, called Major-domo, who commands them. Having arrived in Nombre de Dios and unloaded the gold and silver, they take on merchandise meant for delivery to Panama and from there to Peru, having to leave half of their merchandise at the grange, a place close to said Chagres River, because the barges—unless they are lightened—cannot go upstream on account of its violent current and swiftness. To this end they have to be pushed with poles so that laden with the treasures mentioned above, they need only six to seven hours to come downstream while, on the other hand, it takes them four to five days to go back upstream.

*f. 107*

## COM̃E LES FEMMES YNDIENNES SONT EN PAINE D'ENFFANT (HOW THE INDIAN WOMEN SUFFER LABOR PAINS)

When the Indian women are in labor, the Indian men gather with their musical instruments and walk around the house called "la bouhie," dancing, making as much noise as possible and singing in a loud voice, saying that by this means the woman's pain will go away.

*f. 108*

## COM̃E LES YNDIENS REUIENNENT DELA CARBOUTE AUTREM[ENT] DIT LEBOIS (HOW THE INDIANS RETURN FROM "LA CARBOUTE," ALSO CALLED FOREST)

The Indians coming back from the hunt bring wild pigs as food for their wives after they have given birth to their children, saying that such meat is the best and most nourishing to be found in the Indies.

*f. 109*

## COM̃E LES YNDES BOUCQUANE OU ROTISSENT LE POISSON ET LA CHAIR (HOW THE INDIANS SMOKE OR ROAST FISH AND MEAT)

The Indians make a big fire and when they see the wood turning to charcoal, they take four wooden forks, drive them into the earth and lay several sticks across the forks at a foot and a half above the fire. Then they spread out their fish and meat upon it and when they feel the heat of the fire, the smoke of the fat dropping into the fire smokes or roasts the meat and the fish which are good eating. They turn them often for fear of burning them and when the meat and fish are cooked, they have the color of a red herring.

*f. 110*

## COM̃E LES YNDIENNES VONT LAUER LEURS ENFANS A LA MER QUAND JL EST LA PLAINE LUNE (HOW THE INDIAN WOMEN WASH THEIR CHILDREN IN THE SEA WHEN THE MOON IS FULL)

The Indian women take their children to the sea and wash them. The mother holds one by the hand and the other climbs on her back. They scrub them well so that they have no skin sores or itch and they are clean all over their bodies. The Indian women swim like fish in the sea.

*f. 111–111v*

## COM̃E LES YNDIENS ONT ORDINAIREM[ENT] DES JLLUSIONS DU MALING ESPRIT (HOW THE INDIANS USUALLY HAVE VISIONS OF THE EVIL SPIRIT)

The Indians are much tormented at night by visions of the Evil Spirit whom they call in their language "Athoua." They do not dare leave their houses at night—only when day has come—and this is because they have no belief nor education and do not worship anything like the peoples of Barbary, Guinea, and Brasil. Sleeping one day in an Indian's house and leaving it at night, he begged me to go back into the house, saying that he sees Athoua—equal to the Devil. Asking me the next morning the reason for my fearlessness and boldness, I answered him that he must believe in the crucified Jesus Christ up above who would deliver him of all his diabolical visions if he firmly believes in him. Hearing this, he told me that the one up high was not good; he only sent cold, rain, and scorching heat while the one down on earth was good to them, giving them their daily food like bread, wine, meat, fish, fruits and other goods from the soil itself and that when they die they are buried there. Whereupon I answered that God alone is the creator who created heaven and earth and warms it and makes the fruits come out thanks to which they have their nourishment.

*f. 112*

## COMME LA VIGNE CROIST AUX YNDES (HOW THE VINEYARD GROWS IN THE INDIES)

The Indians plant vineyards in the form of a vinearbor. They are only permitted to plant them in their gardens and not elsewhere. Besides neither the Spaniards nor the Indians are permitted to plant them in abundance and, in like manner, olive trees on account of the high tribute which the King of Spain is collecting from it. Inasmuch as the Spaniards bring in a great quantity of wine from the Canary Islands and oil from Spain which is their best trading merchandise. Trade, therefore, would be without profit to them if the Indians were permitted to plant vineyards and olive trees except in the form seen above, the earth being so fertile that in every season one finds good-tasting fruit in the vineyards.

### f. 113
### COME LES YNDIENS PROCEDENT A LEURS ALLIANCES ET MARIAGES-LES VNGS AUEC LES AUTRES (HOW THE INDIANS MAKE THEIR ALLIANCES AND MARRIAGES WITH EACH OTHER)

The "Le goric," meaning young man, goes to the "bouie" where the house of the father and "La goricque," the daughter whom he loves, are, taking all his equipment, namely his canoe or boat, bow, arrows, "chichorne," or fish-nets. Making his reverence to the father and the daughter, he says "Hai Hai," which means how are you? After having done that, he leaves his whole equipment and utensils in the house and goes away to sleep in a hammock or bed and to rest until the next morning. At daybreak he picks up his bow and arrows to hunt in the wood and having found his prey, takes it to the house, giving it to his beloved or sweetheart to please her and make her cook it. He does not drink or eat in the house before having brought meat and venison in abundance, and he brings as much as possible to show that he works hard to provide well for himself, his wife and family.

### f. 114
### COME LYNDIEN VIENT DU BOIS APPORTANT SA PROIE EN LA MAISON DE SA BIEN AIMEE (HOW THE INDIAN RETURNS FROM THE WOODS CARRYING HIS PREY TO THE HOUSE OF HIS BELOVED)

The next morning the Indian returning from the woods takes his prey to the house, drinking and eating there with the father and mother of his sweetheart in celebration of the alliance regarding his marriage to the daughter.

### f. 115
### COME LINDIEN SEN VA A LA PESCHERIE (HOW THE INDIAN GOES FISHING)

The Indian takes his nets to go fishing and, having caught some, carries his catch to the house of his fiancée to please her. There is plenty of it and it is quite big. They begin to enjoy the great number of fish he brought to the house.

### f. 116
### COME LES YNDIENS SEXERCENT A FAIRE DES RETZ-POUR PESCHER DU POISSON (HOW THE INDIANS LABOR TO MAKE FISHING NETS)

The Indian has such particular virtue that he makes with his hands fishing nets as well as hammocks which are beds for sleeping. They are so skilled that one could not show them any work which they could not do.

### f. 117–117v
### COME LES MESSAGERS YNDIENS VONT PORTER LETTRES PAR LE PAIS (HOW THE INDIAN MESSENGERS CARRY LETTERS ALL OVER THE COUNTRY)

The Indian messengers carry letters far into the country where the Spaniards cannot go on foot. These travelers are given partridges and other game-birds as presents for the Governors to whom packets of letters are sent from the fleet of ships arriving in the Indies to keep them informed. These letters are carried on a stick the end of which is split, and which they hold in their hand. By this means, they pass rivers (swimming across) without wetting the letters. They also have a gourd in which they place the letters, sealing it with wax to keep the water out. Having passed the river, they take out the letters and put them back at the end of the stick. This way, when they find some Indians on their way, these do not dare come near the messenger carrying the letters because he gives them to understand that it is a ghost he carries. When the messenger arrives at the place he has been sent to and has presented the letters together with the game and other things given him and when it is found that a partridge is missing and that he has not presented the contents of the letters, the Lord or Governor to whom these things were sent asks the messenger regarding the missing object. Then the Indian asks him who told him about the missing things and he answers that his letters are a ghost who has revealed it to him, a thing which he [the Indian] firmly believes.

## f. 118
### HINDE FESANTDVFEV (THE INDIAN MAKING A FIRE)

A certain wood is found in the Indies which is very beautiful and yellow in color. They make a hole in the middle of the tree trunk and, taking a stick with cotton, they place it in the hole. By forcefully rubbing the stick with the cotton between their hands against the wood, a fire is started in the cotton.

## f. 119
### COMME LES YNDIENS FILLENT LE COTON (HOW THE INDIANS SPIN THE COTTON)

The Indians take the cotton in their hand with a spindle and twist it on their thighs with great diligence and speed, working with their hands. They will spin half a pound per day and make linen from it with which they clothe themselves.

## f. 120
### CANAV DE COI LES HINDES VONT ALA PAICHERIE ET COMME JLZ PESCHENT LE POISSON (THE CANOE WITH WHICH THE INDIANS GO FISHING AND HOW THEY CATCH FISH)

They go to the sea with their canoe and fishing-line, attaching the line to one side of the canoe. This done, they take their fishing lines and place one over their ears and the other in their mouth. Then, feeling that the fish is caught, they quickly pull in their fishing line and the fish with their hands.

## f. 121
### LA MAÑIERE ET FACON DE JARDINER ET PLANTER DES YNDIENS (THE MANNER AND STYLE OF GARDENING AND PLANTING OF THE INDIANS)

The Indian making his garden sows several kinds of seeds for his food to make it appear that he is working hard and also to please his fiancée and sufficient to feed his wife and children, the soil being so fertile as to bear fruit all the time.

## f. 122
### COME LINDIEN VIENT DUBOIS APPORTANT MANIL (HOW THE INDIAN RETURNS FROM THE WOODS CARRYING MANIL)

Manil is a root from which bread is made which is called Cassava. He brings anything he can find in the woods which is good to eat, as for instance black snakes and other things for his nourishment.

## f. 123
### COME LINDIEN VIENT DU BOIS CHERCHER DES FRUITZ (HOW THE INDIAN RETURNS FROM THE WOODS LOOKING FOR FRUIT)

The Indian returning from the woods brings all kinds of fruit which he can find as nourishment for himself, his wife and family. He carries as much as he possibly can.

## f. 124–124v
### COME LINDIEN AIANT FAICT FIN DE SON TRAUAIL PO[UR] SATIFAIRE ET CONTENTER SA BIEN AIMEE SE JOIGNENT ENSEMBLE EN MARIAGE APPRES LA REMONSTRA[NCE] FAICTE PAR LE PERE DELA FILLE COMME ORRES CY APPRES (HOW THE INDIAN, AFTER FINISHING HIS WORK OF SATISFYING AND PLEASING HIS FIANCÉE, GETS MARRIED AFTER A DEMONSTRATION MADE BY THE FATHER OF THE BRIDE AS YOU WILL HEAR HEREAFTER)

The Indian, having worked as much as possible to give pleasure to his fiancée, dresses himself as magnificently as he can and returns to the house of the father of the bride and points out to him the hard work he is capable of and the good will he has to nourish them well. Seeing this, the father demonstrates to the daughter in his presence, telling her, "You need this young man. He will feed you well. You see that he brings a lot of good things for us to eat; he works hard at fishing as well as at catching wild animals; he plants, gathers fruit and firewood, in short, everything needed to feed the whole house." After having made this demonstration, the father points out similarly to the young man how well his daughter works at baking bread and dressing meat which she will cook in the cask, also called pot.

After all these demonstrations have been made, they are joined in marriage in the house of the father. When they are married, father and mother no longer want to work and customarily their children feed them. There is only one tribe in each village and they do not permit others, not from their tribe, to live in this village. They choose the oldest one whom they call Cacique who is like a king and whom they obey in everything. And when their land no longer bears fruit or is tired of producing, they leave it and go to live in another place where they cultivate the land and where they know there is fresh water. Then after three or four years, they return to their first land where they settle down as they had done before.